Spiritual Warfare Workbook:
A Practical Guide to Victory in Christ

Dr. Rosemica D. Bonhomme

Dedication

This workbook is dedicated to my omnipotent God and Savior, Jesus Christ, who has never failed me. I also dedicate it to my wonderful family. In particular, I honor my deceased father, Isaac Damier, who worked tirelessly to bring me and my siblings to the USA for a better life. I am grateful to my mother for her unconditional love and invaluable advice that only a mother can provide.

Additionally, I want to extend my dedication to my spiritual family, who are truly unique and irreplaceable, as well as to all believers who desire to stand firm in Christ, overcome the attacks of the enemy, and walk daily in spiritual victory. May this resource strengthen, equip, and empower you to live boldly in the full armor of God. To God be the glory, now and forever. Amen!

Table of Contents

Foreword

One of the greatest needs in the church today is a return to the Scriptures as the foundation for Christian living. We live in a time of war that is both visible and unseen—affecting our homes, workplaces, governments, and even the church. In every generation, God raises voices not merely to speak, but to equip, warn, and strengthen His people. This book is a response to the countless believers and seekers around the world who are searching for clarity, strength, and victory in the midst of their daily battles.

Spiritual Warfare Workbook: A Practical Guide to Victory in Christ is not a book born out of curiosity, theory, or spiritual enthusiasm. It is the fruit of prayer, spiritual discernment, and obedience to a divine assignment. It addresses the reality of spiritual warfare-something many believers face daily yet often lack the teaching, understanding, or tools to confront.

The word of God clearly teaches that our struggle is not against flesh and blood, but against spiritual forces of evil in the heavenly realms. Yet too often, believers attempt to fight spiritual battles with natural methods—leading to frustration, exhaustion, and unnecessary defeat. This workbook gently yet firmly redirects the believer back to the vital truth: victory has already been secured in Christ, but it must be understood, applied, and enforced through faith.

What makes this workbook unique is its balance. It is deeply rooted in Scripture, yet practical in application. It neither magnifies the enemy nor ignores him; instead, it magnifies Christ—His authority, His finished work on the cross, and the believer's rightful position in Him. Through teaching, reflection, prayer, and application, readers are guided to recognize spiritual attacks, stand firm in faith, and engage in spiritual warfare from a position of victory rather than fear.

I have witnessed Rosemica's spiritual journey—her devotion to prayer, love for God's Word, and genuine burden for God's people. This work reflects not only sound doctrine, but also a heart that longs to see believers healed, restored, and empowered to live in the victory Christ provides. It has been written with pastoral care, spiritual maturity, and a deep sensitivity to the leading of the Holy Spirit.

I believe this book will be a blessing to individuals, families, prayer groups, and churches. It will strengthen marriages, sharpen spiritual discernment, revive prayer lives, and remind believers that they are not powerless, but more than conquerors in Christ.

As you engage with this workbook, I encourage you to approach it prayerfully. Allow the Holy Spirit to reveal truth, bring conviction where needed, and impart strength for the journey ahead. This is not merely a workbook to be read—it is a powerful guide for daily living.

May God use this work to awaken your spiritual awareness, break strongholds, and raise up believers who stand firm in faith, walk boldly in authority, and live fully in the victory found in Christ Jesus.

In His service,

Farile Erase

Pastor, Church Educator, Family Therapist, Marriage Coach

Spiritual Warfare Workbook:

A Practical Guide to Victory in Christ

Introduction

"Finally, my brethren, be strong in the Lord and in the power of His might" (Ephesians 6:10, KJV).

Spiritual warfare is not a myth, a metaphor, or a concept reserved for only a few believers. It is a **daily reality** in the life of every follower of Jesus Christ. Whether we acknowledge it or not, there is a very real enemy seeking to destroy lives, divide families, weaken faith, and prevent the purposes of God from being fulfilled.

This workbook was born out of a passion to **equip the Body of Christ** with the truth, tools, and confidence needed to stand firm in the face of spiritual resistance. Too many believers are defeated simply because they are unaware of the battle they are in—or ill-equipped to fight it.

What Is Spiritual Warfare?

Spiritual warfare refers to the **invisible battle** between the Kingdom of God and the forces of darkness. It plays out in the spiritual realm but manifests in our lives, relationships, emotions, decisions, and ministries.

The good news is this: **Jesus has already won the victory.** As believers, we do not fight for victory—we fight *from* victory. But we must still take up the spiritual weapons God provides, walk in discernment, and remain grounded in His Word.

Why This Workbook?

This workbook is a **biblical, practical, and personal** guide designed to:

- help you understand your **identity and authority in Christ,**

- teach you how to **put on the full armor of God,**

- equip you to **resist the devil and walk in freedom,**

- offer **daily devotionals, prayers,** and **group discussion tools, and**

- lead you into a deeper experience of **deliverance, intercession, and victory.**

Whether you are a new believer or a seasoned leader, this workbook is for you. It is meant to be studied alone, taught in small groups, or shared in prayer ministries.

How to Use This Workbook

- **Individually**: Work through each chapter with your Bible open, take notes, reflect, and apply.

- **With a Group**: Use the teaching notes and discussion guides to facilitate group study and prayer.

- **As a Leader**: Adapt the chapters for sermons, classes, or deliverance ministry training.

"The weapons of our warfare are not carnal but mighty through God to the pulling down of strongholds" (2 Corinthians 10:4).

Let's begin.

Chapter 1:
The Reality of the Spiritual Realm

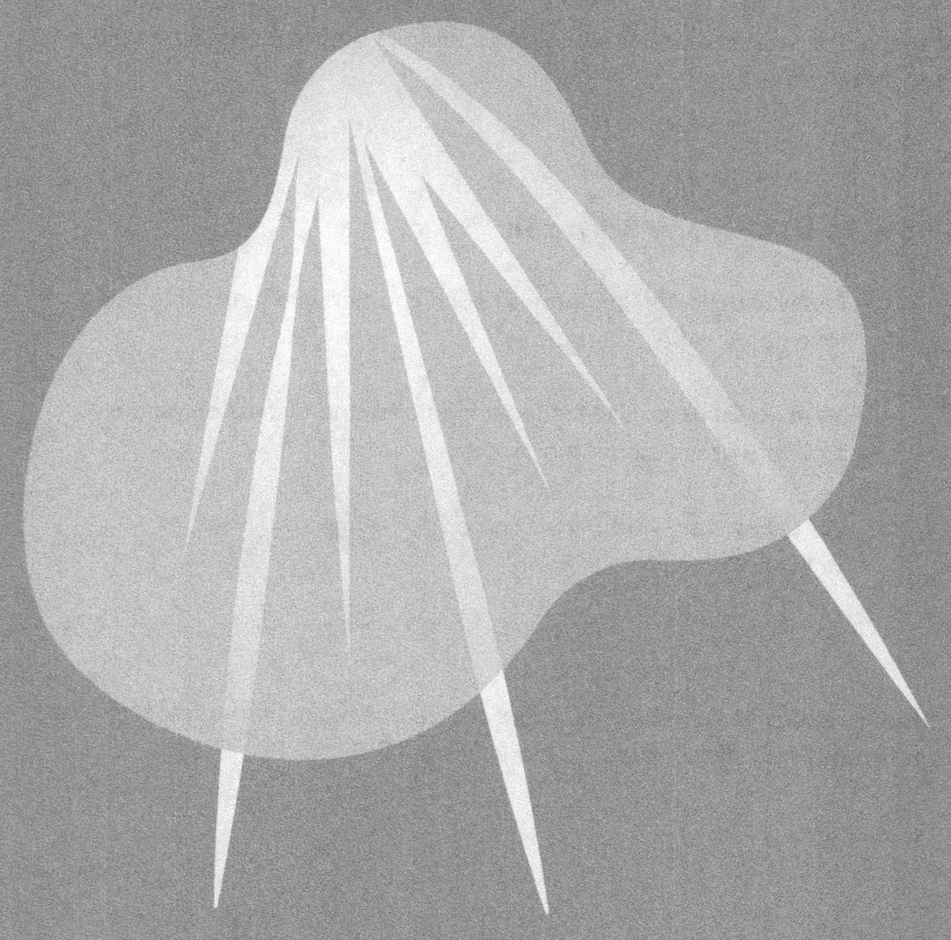

Key Scriptures

- *Ephesians 6:12 (NKJV)—"For we do not wrestle against flesh and blood, but against principalities, against powers, against the rulers of the darkness of this age, against spiritual hosts of wickedness in the heavenly places."*

- *2 Kings 6:17 (NIV)—"And Elisha prayed, 'Open his eyes, Lord, so that he may see.' Then the Lord opened the servant's eyes, and he looked and saw the hills full of horses and chariots of fire all around Elisha."*

Overview

The spiritual realm is more real than what we see with our natural eyes. Throughout the Bible, the spiritual realm is unveiled in moments of divine encounter and prophetic vision. It is a realm that coexists with the natural world and is populated by angels, demons, and the power of God. Understanding its presence is foundational to spiritual warfare.

Examples of the Spiritual Realm in Scripture

1. Creation and the Fall of Satan

- **Isaiah 14:12–15** and **Ezekiel 28:12–19** describe the fall of Lucifer from heaven. Once a glorious angel, his rebellion led to his expulsion along with a third of the angels.

2. Angelic Visitation and Protection

- **Genesis 28:12**—Jacob dreams of a ladder reaching from earth to heaven with angels ascending and descending.

- **Psalm 91:11**—*"For He will command His angels concerning you to guard you in all your ways."*

- **Daniel 6:22**—An angel shuts the mouths of lions in the den.

3. Spiritual Battles and Visions

- **Daniel 10:12-13**—Daniel's prayers are delayed because of warfare between angelic and demonic forces.

- **Revelation 12:7-9**—Michael and his angels fight against the dragon (Satan) and his angels.

4. Jesus and the Spiritual Realm

- **Matthew 4:1-11**—Jesus is tempted by Satan in the wilderness.

- **Luke 10:18**—"I saw Satan fall like lightning from heaven."

- **Colossians 2:15**—Jesus disarmed principalities and powers through the Cross.

5. The Early Church and Spiritual Encounters

- **Acts 5:15-16**—People are healed and delivered from demonic spirits.

- **Acts 16:16-18**—Paul casts a spirit of divination out of a girl.

Theological Insights

- **The spiritual realm is real**: It impacts natural events, personal decisions, and cultural movements.

- **We are seated with Christ**: Believers are given spiritual authority in the heavenly realms (Ephesians 2:6).

- **God's angelic army is present**: There are more for us than against us (2 Kings 6:16).

Practical Application

- Pray for spiritual eyes to be opened.

- Engage the spiritual realm through prayer, worship, and the Word.

- Stay grounded in biblical truth to avoid fear or mysticism.

Expanded Study

1. The Bible reveals two realms: the visible (physical) and the invisible (spiritual).

- The physical realm is what we experience with our five senses—what we see, hear, touch, taste, and smell. But Scripture makes clear that there is also a spiritual realm that is just as real, though unseen.

- **2 Corinthians 4:18** says, *"We do not look at the things which are seen, but at the things which are not seen. For the things which are seen are temporary, but the things which are not seen are eternal."*

- The visible world is temporary, while the spiritual world is eternal. Many earthly struggles are directly connected to battles being fought in this unseen dimension.

- **Practical Insight:** Believers must not focus only on natural solutions but also invite God's intervention from the spiritual realm.

---

2. Angels and demons are active in the unseen realm (Daniel 10, Revelation 12).

- Angels are ministering spirits sent by God to protect, guide, and strengthen His people (**Hebrews 1:14**).

- Demons, fallen angels who rebelled with Satan, oppose God's purposes and attempt to deceive, oppress, and destroy (John 10:10).

- In **Daniel 10**, the angel Gabriel was delayed twenty-one days by a demonic "prince of Persia" until Michael the archangel came to help. This shows that spiritual conflicts can affect events on earth.

- **Revelation 12** depicts a war in heaven where Satan and his angels fought against Michael and God's angels.

- **Practical Insight:** Spiritual activity is happening all around us, whether we acknowledge it or not. Christians must remember they are not alone—God has assigned heavenly help.

3. Spiritual battles often manifest in areas such as temptation, oppression, fear, sickness, and discouragement.

- Temptation: Satan tempted Jesus in the wilderness (Matthew 4:1–11). Temptation is not random; it's targeted warfare against our weaknesses.

- Oppression: In Acts 10:38, Jesus went about *"healing all who were oppressed by the devil."*

- Fear: Fear is often a tactic of the enemy to paralyze believers from walking in faith (2 Timothy 1:7).

- Sickness: While not all sickness is demonic, Scripture shows cases where sickness was linked to demonic influence (Luke 13:11–16).

- Discouragement: Elijah, after a great victory, fell into despair and wished to die (1 Kings 19:1–4). This shows how spiritual battles can impact emotions and mental health.

- **Practical Insight:** When unusual patterns of temptation, fear, or oppression persist, they may indicate spiritual resistance. These situations require prayer, Scripture, and standing firm in faith.

4. Ignoring the reality of the spiritual realm leaves believers vulnerable.

- When Christians downplay or ignore spiritual warfare, they risk being caught off guard.

- **Hosea 4:6** warns, *"My people are destroyed for lack of knowledge."*

- The enemy thrives in secrecy and deception. By pretending spiritual battles don't exist, believers give him space to operate unchecked.

- Paul warned the Corinthians to remain alert so that *"Satan should take advantage of us; for we are not ignorant of his devices"* (**2 Corinthians 2:11**).

- **Practical Insight:** Knowledge of the spiritual realm equips believers to pray strategically, resist temptation, and protect their homes and families.

Common Signs

- Persistent fear or confusion without clear cause

- Repeated cycles of failure or bondage

- Constant division or strife in families or churches

- Dreams that bring oppression or fear

- An atmosphere of heaviness or despair

Example

A believer constantly felt a heavy presence in their home at night and battled irrational fear. After prayer and dedicating their home to Christ, peace
and freedom replaced fear.

Biblical Example

In 2 Kings 6, Elisha's servant panicked at the sight of a Syrian army. Elisha
prayed, and God opened his eyes to see the mountain full of heavenly
chariots and horses of fire. What looked like certain defeat was actually
surrounded by God's protection.

Reflection Questions

- Do you live with awareness that there is a battle beyond the
  physical? Ask God to open your spiritual eyes.

- How aware are you of the spiritual battle around you?

- In what ways have you experienced the reality of spiritual warfare?

....

....

....

....

....

- How does knowing your authority in Christ affect your confidence in battle?

....

....

....

....

- Do you live with awareness that there is a battle beyond the physical? Ask God to open your spiritual eyes.

....

....

....

....

Exercises

1. **Journal Reflection:** Write about a time when you sensed spiritual opposition in your life. How did you respond? What would you do differently now with this new understanding?

2. **Scripture Meditation:** Spend five minutes daily this week meditating on Ephesians 6:12. Write down any insights or impressions you receive.

3. **Prayer Practice:** Begin each day this week by praying, "Lord, help me see and stand firm against the spiritual battles around me. Fill me with Your strength and wisdom."

Discussion Questions

- Why is it important to understand that our struggle is not "against flesh and blood"?

- How does this perspective change the way we approach difficulties in life?

- What challenges do believers face when accepting the reality of spiritual warfare?

Prayer Guide

- **Prayer for Awareness:**
  "Father, open my eyes to the spiritual battle around me. Help me to recognize the enemy's schemes and stand firm in Your strength."

- ● **Prayer for Identity:**
  "Lord Jesus, remind me daily that I am seated with You in heavenly places, clothed with authority and victory. Help me walk confidently in this truth."

- ● **Prayer for Protection:**
  "Holy Spirit, surround me with Your peace and protection. Shield me from deception, fear, and attacks by the enemy."

Topics Covered

- ● The spiritual realm in Scripture

- ● The fall of Lucifer and the rise of demonic forces

- ● Angels, demons, and their influence in the world today

- ● The role of the believer in spiritual awareness

- ● The two realms: visible (physical) and invisible (spiritual)

- ● The activity of angels and demons

- ● How spiritual battles manifest in everyday life (temptation, fear, oppression, sickness, discouragement)

- ● The danger of ignoring spiritual warfare

- ● The believer's call to awareness and vigilance

Chapter 2:
Understanding the Enemy

Key Scriptures

- *1 Peter 5:8—"Be sober, be vigilant; because your adversary the devil walks about like a roaring lion, seeking whom he may devour."*

Overview

Satan is a defeated enemy, yet he remains a formidable threat. Recognizing his strategies and goals enables effective resistance. His primary tactics include deception, accusation, temptation, and oppression. Although he cannot overpower God's children, he aims to distract, divide, and destroy through lies. Understanding these strategies helps believers identify and resist his attacks.

Expanded Study

Who Is Satan?

Satan, also known as the devil, was originally an angel named Lucifer. He became proud and rebelled against God. Cast out of heaven, he now works to oppose God and His people (Isaiah 14:12–15; Revelation 12:7–9). He is described as a deceiver, tempter, accuser, and enemy of our souls (John 8:44; 1 Peter 5:8).

The Nature of Demons

Demons are fallen angels who followed Satan in his rebellion. They are disembodied spirits who seek to inhabit, influence, or torment human lives (Luke 11:24–26). Their goal is to separate people from God, to create confusion, and to spread spiritual darkness.

Common Strategies of the Enemy:

- **Deception**: Satan is the father of lies (John 8:44). He distorts God's truth to lead people astray.

- **Distraction**: He diverts believers from prayer, Scripture, and God's calling with busyness or worldly pursuits.

- **Discouragement**: He uses shame, failure, and fear to weaken our faith and make us give up.

Knowing Your Weak Points and Guarding Them

Everyone has areas of vulnerability—whether it be pride, fear, lust, insecurity, or anger. Identifying and surrendering these to God through prayer, accountability, and Scripture is key to staying strong in the battle.

Advanced Exploration

1. Satan is real, but he is a defeated foe (Colossians 2:15).

- Many people today downplay Satan as just a symbol of evil, but Scripture makes clear that he is a real spiritual being, the adversary of God and His people.

- Yet, Satan is not equal to God. He is a created being and already defeated through Christ's work on the cross.

- **Colossians 2:15** says, *"Having disarmed principalities and powers, He made a public spectacle of them, triumphing over them in it."*

- This means Satan has lost his legal authority over believers. His power now operates mainly through lies and deception, not absolute control.

- **Practical Insight:** We fight from victory, not for victory. The believer does not need to fear the devil but must remain alert and stand in Christ's authority.

2. His main tactic is deception—twisting God's Word or planting lies (Genesis 3).

- From the beginning, Satan's strategy has been to distort God's Word. In the Garden of Eden, he asked Eve, *"Did God really say...?"* *(Genesis 3:1)*. By twisting God's command, he sowed doubt and deception.

- Jesus described him as *"the father of lies"* *(John 8:44)*. His lies often mix truth with falsehood to confuse and mislead.

- Deception can appear in false teachings, distorted worldviews, and even personal negative thoughts.

- **Practical Insight:** The best defense against deception is knowing Scripture. Just as Jesus responded to temptation with *"It is written..."* *(Matthew 4)*, believers must use God's Word to expose lies.

3. He accuses believers before God (Revelation 12:10).

- One of Satan's names is *"the accuser of the brethren."* Revelation 12:10 says, *"For the accuser of our brethren, who accused them before our God day and night, has been cast down."*

- His accusations often come as condemning thoughts that make believers feel unworthy, unloved, or unforgiven.

- Unlike the Holy Spirit's conviction (which leads to repentance and restoration), Satan's accusations lead to shame and despair.

- **Practical Insight:** Believers can silence the enemy's accusations with the truth of God's Word, especially Romans 8:1: *"There is therefore now no condemnation to those who are in Christ Jesus."*

4. He blinds the minds of unbelievers to keep them from salvation (2 Corinthians 4:4).

- The devil's goal is to prevent people from knowing Christ. **2 Corinthians 4:4** says, *"The god of this age has blinded the minds of unbelievers, so that they cannot see the light of the gospel..."*

- This blinding happens through distractions, false religions, worldly philosophies, pride, or even spiritual apathy.

- Spiritual blindness is not just ignorance; it is an intentional darkening influenced by the enemy.

- **Practical Insight:** Believers must pray for God to open the eyes of unbelievers. Evangelism and intercession are weapons against this spiritual blindness.

5. He seeks to influence culture, families, and individuals through sin and compromise.

- Satan works not only in personal lives but also in society, shaping culture in ways that oppose God's truth.

- Examples include moral compromise, normalization of sin, broken families, and ideologies that reject God.

- Ephesians 2:2 describes unbelievers as following *"the prince of the power of the air, the spirit who now works in the sons of disobedience."*

- By enticing people to compromise—whether in entertainment, relationships, or values—Satan weakens faith and corrupts generations.

- **Practical Insight:** Christians are called to be *"salt and light"*

(Matthew 5: 13 – 16), resisting cultural pressures and standing firm in holiness while influencing society for Christ.

Common Signs

- Persistent feelings of condemnation despite repentance

- Confusion about truth versus lies

- Constant temptation in weak areas

- Division in relationships

- Fear, shame, or guilt that paralyzes spiritual growth

Example

A believer constantly battled the thought, "God doesn't love you anymore." This lie made them withdraw from prayer. Once they recognized the source, they resisted the lie with Romans 8:38–39, and peace returned.

Biblical Example

In Matthew 4, Satan tempted Jesus with food, power, and recognition. Each time, Jesus responded with Scripture: *"It is written..."* His example shows that victory comes through knowing and applying God's Word.

Practical Insight

The enemy has no new tricks—his tactics are the same as in the beginning: lies, temptation, and distraction. Recognizing the lie is the first step; replacing it with truth is the second.

Practical Application

- Pray for spiritual eyes to be opened.

- Engage the spiritual realm through prayer, worship, and the Word.

- Stay grounded in biblical truth to avoid fear or mysticism.

Reflection Questions

- What lies or deceptions have you noticed the enemy using against you?

- Can you identify personal weaknesses that the enemy might exploit?

- How does understanding the enemy's tactics change your approach to spiritual warfare?

- Which of the enemy's strategies have you seen in your own life? How can you resist him through God's Word?

Exercises

1. **Personal Inventory:** Write down areas in your life where you feel vulnerable to temptation or discouragement. Pray over each area, asking God for strength and protection.

2. **Scripture Defense:** Memorize and declare aloud James 4:7—"*Submit yourselves, then, to God. Resist the devil, and he will flee from you.*" Use this verse whenever you feel under attack.

3. **Prayer of Confession and Guarding:** Pray daily, confessing any known/unknown sins and asking God to strengthen your defenses in areas of weakness.

Discussion Questions

- How can we distinguish between when the enemy is using deception and when we are facing natural challenges?

- What practical steps can you take to "know your weak points" and guard them effectively?

- How do community and accountability play a role in spiritual protection?

Prayer Guide

- **Prayer for Revelation:**
  "Lord, reveal to me the enemy's schemes and any areas where I am vulnerable. Help me to stand firm and resist his attacks."

- **Prayer for Strength:**
  "Father, empower me with Your Spirit to overcome temptation, discouragement, and distraction. Help me live in freedom and victory."

- **Prayer for Protection:**
  "Jesus, cover me with Your blood and surround me with Your angels. Keep me safe from all spiritual harm."

Topics Covered

- Who is Satan?

- The nature of demons

- Common strategies of the enemy (deception, distraction, discouragement)

- Knowing your weak points and guarding them

- The identity and tactics of Satan

- Lies, accusations, and temptations

- Victory through Christ and the Word

- Replacing lies with truth

- Living alert but unafraid

Chapter 3:
Our Identity in
Christ

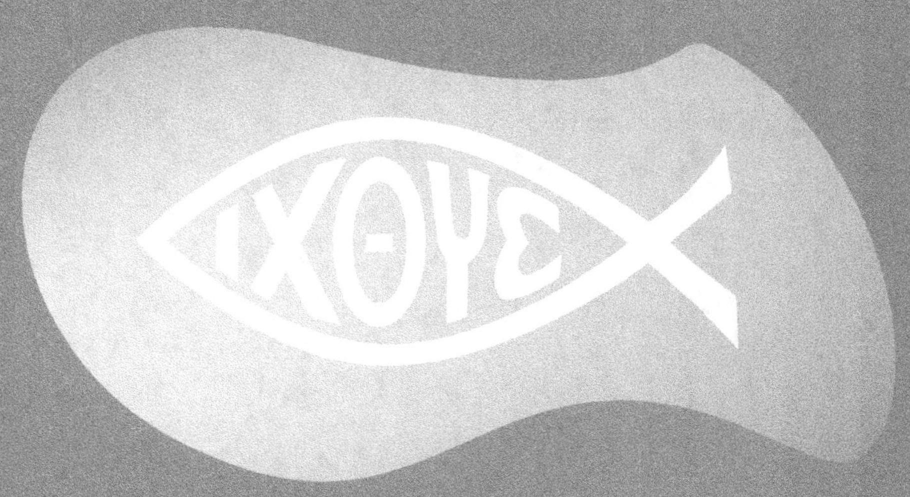

Key Scriptures

- *2 Corinthians 5:17—"Therefore, if anyone is in Christ, he is a new creation; old things have passed away; behold, all things have become new."*

Overview

Knowing your identity in Christ is crucial for winning spiritual battles. Your identity is the foundation of your authority, confidence, and freedom. Understanding who you are in Christ empowers you in spiritual warfare. The enemy tries to distort your self-image, but Christ has redefined you as loved, forgiven, and victorious. Embracing this truth is key to victory in spiritual battles.

This chapter dives deeply into four foundational truths about our new life in Christ.

Expanded Study

1. You Are a New Creation

When you receive Jesus as Lord and Savior, you are not simply improved; you are reborn. Your old sinful nature is crucified with Christ (Galatians 2:20), and you are made spiritually alive. This transformation includes a new heart, new desires, and a new standing before God.

- **Romans 6:4**—*We were buried with Him through baptism into death, and raised to walk in newness of life.*

- **Ezekiel 36:26**—*"I will give you a new heart and put a new spirit in you."*

Practical Insight: Stop identifying yourself by past sins or failures. Confess out loud: "I am a new creation in Christ—my past does not define me."

2. You Are Seated with Christ in Heavenly Places

Being "seated with Christ" (Ephesians 2:6) is a positional truth. It means you share in Jesus's victory and reign. You are not fighting from a place of defeat, but from a place of spiritual authority.

- **Ephesians 1:20–21**—Christ is seated far above all principality and power.

- **Colossians 3:1–3**—You are raised with Christ; set your mind on things above.

Practical Insight: Begin each day by affirming your heavenly position. It shifts your mindset from fear to victory.

3. The Authority of the Believer

Jesus gave His followers authority to trample on all the power of the enemy (Luke 10:19). This authority is based not on our merit, but on Christ's victory over sin, death, and Satan.

- **Mark 16:17**—*"In My name, they will cast out demons..."*

- **James 4:7**—Submit to God, resist the devil, and he will flee.

Practical Insight: Exercise your authority by speaking Scripture, rebuking the enemy in Jesus's name, and praying boldly. Authority is most effective when rooted in obedience and intimacy with God.

4. Living from Your Heavenly Identity

Your identity is not based on emotions, achievements, or the opinions of others. You are a child of God, an heir with Christ, a citizen of heaven, and the righteousness of God (Romans 8:17; Philippians 3:20; 2 Corinthians 5:21).

Living from this identity involves:

- **Renewing your mind** with truth (Romans 12:2)

- **Walking in the Spirit** (Galatians 5:16)

- **Pursuing holiness** (1 Peter 1:15–16)

Practical Insight: Journal affirmations of who you are in Christ. Speak them aloud during prayer. Let your identity shape your choices and reactions.

Empowered by Identity

1. In Christ, believers are sons and daughters of God (John 1:12).

- Salvation doesn't just rescue us from sin; it brings us into God's family.

- **John 1:12** says, *"But as many as received Him, to them He gave the right to become children of God, to those who believe in His name."*

- This adoption into God's family gives us the privilege of calling Him Abba, Father (Romans 8:15).

- Satan wants us to forget this identity because when we see ourselves only as weak or unworthy, we hesitate to exercise authority.

- **Practical Insight:** Spiritual warfare is fought with the confidence of being God's child, not a fearful servant. Sons and daughters fight from relationship, not religion.

---

2. We are no longer slaves to sin but free (Romans 6:18).

- Before Christ, sin ruled us; we were captives to its power. But in salvation, sin's mastery was broken.

- **Romans 6:18** declares, *"And having been set free from sin, you became slaves of righteousness."*

- Freedom doesn't mean we never struggle, but that sin no longer has dominion (Romans 6:14). We now have the power, through the Spirit, to choose righteousness.

- Satan often tries to deceive believers into thinking they are still bound by their old habits, failures, or addictions.

- **Practical Insight:** When the enemy reminds you of your past, declare your freedom in Christ. You are no longer chained—you are free to live holy.

---

3. Our worth comes from God's declaration, not our failures.

- The enemy whispers shame: "You failed; therefore, you are worthless." But God defines our worth, not our mistakes.

- Scripture says we are *"fearfully and wonderfully made"* (Psalm 139:14) and *"God's workmanship, created in Christ Jesus for good works"* (Ephesians 2:10).

- When Christ died on the cross, He declared our value—worth His own blood (1 Peter 1:18–19).

- **Practical Insight:** Identity in warfare means rejecting condemnation and embracing God's truth: "I am redeemed, forgiven, chosen, and loved." This mindset disarms the enemy's accusations.

---

4. Knowing identity builds confidence in prayer and warfare.

- Confidence in warfare is not arrogance but assurance. Hebrews 4:16 says, *"Let us therefore come boldly to the throne of grace, that we may obtain mercy and find grace to help in time of need."*

- When we know we are children of God, free from sin's control, and valuable in His sight, we pray with boldness instead of fear.

- Satan's schemes often lose their grip the moment believers realize who they are in Christ.

- **Practical Insight:** Identity fuels authority. The more you know who you are in Christ, the less you will believe the lies of the enemy.

Common Signs

- Struggles with insecurity or low self-worth

- Believing labels from past failures

- Comparing oneself constantly to others

- Difficulty believing God truly loves or forgives

Example

A young man believed he was "a failure" because of past mistakes. After meditating on Romans 8:1, he realized condemnation was broken, and he began to live with confidence in God's forgiveness.

Biblical Example

Gideon hid in fear, calling himself "the least." But God called him a **mighty warrior** (Judges 6). His true identity was based on God's declaration, not his opinion.

Practical Insight

If the enemy can keep you confused about who you are, he can keep you powerless. Identity is not how you feel; it's who God says you are.

Key Memory Verses

- 2 Corinthians 5:17

- Ephesians 2:6

- Luke 10:19

- Romans 12:2

Reflection Questions

- How does knowing you are a new creation change your view of yourself and your battles?

- In what ways can you live more consistently from your heavenly position?

....

....

....

....

....

- How do you currently exercise your authority in Christ? Where could you grow?

....

....

....

....

- Do you live like a new creation or like your old self? What would change if you truly believed you were seated with Christ in victory?

....

....

....

....

- Do you believe what God says about who you are? How can you walk in that identity this week?

....

....

....

....

....

Exercises:

1. **Identity Declaration:** Write out a personal declaration based on key identity Scriptures (e.g., "I am a new creation," "I am seated with Christ," "I have authority over the enemy"). Speak it aloud daily.

2. **Authority in Action:** Practice praying over a situation in your life, claiming the authority Jesus has given you to overcome. Journal what you sense God doing.

3. **Heavenly Mindset:** Take five minutes daily to meditate on Ephesians 2:6, imagining yourself seated with Christ and empowered by His presence.

Discussion Questions

- What are some lies you've believed about yourself that need to be replaced with your true identity?

- How can living from your heavenly position impact your daily walk and spiritual battles?

- What are practical ways to strengthen your faith in exercising spiritual authority?

Prayer Guide

- **Prayer for Identity:**
  "Lord, help me to fully grasp who I am in You—a new creation, redeemed and empowered. Teach me to live in that truth."

- **Prayer for Transformation:**
  "Holy Spirit, renew my mind daily. Help me reject the enemy's lies and embrace my identity in Christ."

Topics Covered

- You are a new creation

- You are seated with Christ in heavenly places

- Authority of the believer

- Living from your heavenly identity

- The identity and tactics of Satan

- Lies, accusations, and temptations

- Victory through Christ and the Word

- Replacing lies with truth

- Living alert but unafraid

Chapter 4:
Authority of the Believer

Key Scriptures

- ***Luke 10:19**—"Behold, I give you the authority to trample on serpents and scorpions, and over all the power of the enemy, and nothing shall by any means hurt you."*

Overview

Believers are not helpless victims. Jesus gave His disciples power to trample over the forces of darkness. The believer's authority is a spiritual inheritance through Christ. We are empowered to overcome the enemy, speak God's Word boldly, and act in alignment with heaven. This chapter explores how to use that authority wisely and effectively.

Expanded Study

1. Delegated Authority Through Christ

Jesus holds all authority in heaven and on earth (Matthew 28:18), and He has delegated that authority to His Church. This means believers act not in their own name, but in the name of Jesus. This delegation is legal, spiritual, and powerful.

- **Matthew 28:18-20**—*"All authority in heaven and on earth has been given to Me... therefore go."*

- **John 14:12-14**—*"Whoever believes in Me will do the works I have been doing..."*

Practical Insight: Just as a police officer's badge represents governmental power, your use of Jesus's name represents divine power and backing.

2. How to Use Spiritual Authority in Prayer and Warfare

Authority is exercised by:

- **Speaking the Word of God**—As Jesus did in the wilderness (Matthew 4).

- **Praying in Jesus's name**—This isn't a formula but a position of alignment with His will.

- **Commanding spirits to leave**—Like the apostles did in Acts.

- **Interceding with confidence**—Knowing heaven hears and responds.

Scripture Support

- **Mark 11:23-24**—Speak to the mountain and believe.

- **Acts 16:18**—Paul commands a spirit of divination to leave.

3. Binding and Loosing

Jesus gave believers authority to bind and loose (Matthew 16:19; 18:18). This means:

- **Binding** = to forbid or restrict (e.g., demonic influence, lies, fear).

- **Loosing** = to permit or release (e.g., truth, healing, peace).

Practical Example: "In Jesus's name, I bind every spirit of confusion and fear. I loose the peace and wisdom of God over this situation."

Scripture Support

- **Matthew 18:18**—*"Whatever you bind on earth will be bound in heaven..."*

- **Isaiah 61:1**—Jesus proclaims liberty to captives.

4. When to Stand and When to Flee

There is wisdom in knowing when to stand firm and when to flee:

- **Stand firm**: When confronting spiritual attacks, temptations, or injustice (Ephesians 6:13; James 4:7)

- **Flee**: When faced with sin that tempts the flesh. Flee youthful lusts (2 Timothy 2:22), idolatry (1 Corinthians 10:14), and sexual immorality (1 Corinthians 6:18).

Advanced Exploration

1. Authority comes from being in Christ (Matthew 28:18-19).

- Authority is not earned by human effort; it flows directly from Jesus.

- After His resurrection, Jesus declared in **Matthew 28:18-19**: *"All authority in heaven and on earth has been given to me. Therefore, go and make disciples..."*

- Notice the order: Jesus first established His own supreme authority then delegated that authority to His followers.

- Believers do not fight Satan in their own power but in the name and authority of Christ.

- **Practical Insight:** Whenever you pray, resist temptation, or stand against the enemy, you do so not in your name but in the name of Jesus. Just as a police officer carries authority because of the badge—not personal strength—we stand strong because of Christ.

---

2. Believers are seated with Christ in heavenly places (Ephesians 2:6).

- Salvation not only rescues us from sin but also elevates our spiritual position.

- **Ephesians 2:6** declares: *"And God raised us up with Christ and seated us with Him in the heavenly realms in Christ Jesus."*

- To be "seated with Christ" means sharing in His authority, victory, and dominion. Spiritually, we stand above principalities, not beneath them.

- This seating is not future; it is a present reality. It gives believers confidence to pray with authority and to resist demonic attacks.

- **Practical Insight:** The devil wants believers to feel defeated and powerless. But when we remember where we are seated—in Christ above all powers—we pray and live with confidence, not fear.

---

3. Authority is exercised through prayer, declaration, and obedience.

- **Prayer**: Prayer is the channel through which believers release God's authority into situations. Jesus taught us to pray, *"Your kingdom come, Your will be done, on earth as it is in heaven"* (Matthew 6:10). Prayer enforces heaven's authority over earth.

- **Declaration**: Speaking God's Word out loud is a weapon. Jesus defeated Satan's temptations by declaring, *"It is written"* (Matthew 4:4,7,10). Declarations align our words with God's truth and silence lies.

- **Obedience**: Authority flows from submission to God. James 4:7 teaches, *"Submit to God. Resist the devil, and he will flee from you."* Without submission, authority loses its power.

- **Practical Insight:** Authority is not about shouting louder at the enemy but about standing in faith, speaking God's Word, and living in obedience. A life aligned with God carries weight in the spiritual realm.

4. The enemy is already defeated but seeks to intimidate.

- Satan knows his end—Revelation 20:10 says he will be thrown into the lake of fire. But until then, he operates through intimidation, fear, and deception.

- **1 Peter 5:8** describes him as a roaring lion—not a conquering one—seeking who he may devour. Lions roar to create fear and paralyze their prey before attacking.

- Though defeated, Satan tries to convince believers that they are powerless. He magnifies problems to overshadow God's promises.

- **Practical Insight:** Never negotiate with intimidation. When the enemy roars with fear, respond with faith. Speak Scripture, stand firm, and remember he has no authority over you unless you yield it.

Common Signs

- Fear when confronting evil or oppression

- Feeling powerless in spiritual struggles

- Reluctance to use Jesus's name boldly

Example

A family experienced disturbances in their home. Once they prayed with authority in Jesus's name and declared peace, the disturbances ceased.

Biblical Example

In Acts 16, Paul commanded a spirit of divination to leave a slave girl in Jesus's name. The spirit left immediately, showing the authority believers carry.

Practical Insight

- Authority is like a badge—power isn't in the person but in the name they represent.

- Use the authority of Jesus with confidence, not hesitation.

- Stand firm in truth and prayer when under spiritual oppression.

- Flee situations where your spiritual footing is weak or compromised.

Key Memory Verses:

- Luke 10:19

- Matthew 18:18

- James 4:7

- 2 Timothy 2:22

Reflection Questions:

- How do you understand your delegated authority in Christ?

- Can you recall a time you exercised spiritual authority effectively?

- How do you discern when to stand firm and when to withdraw?

- Where have you been passive when God has given you authority? Where do you need discernment to stand or to flee?

- Have you been using your authority or living in fear? Speak and act with confidence in the power of Jesus.

- Why do many believers hesitate to use their authority?

- How does knowing your position in Christ give confidence?

....

....

....

....

....

Exercises

1. **Authority Prayer Practice:** Write and pray a short prayer declaring your authority over a specific area of struggle or attack.

2. **Binding and Loosing Exercise:** Identify an area in your life or community needing spiritual intervention. Pray to bind the enemy's work and loose God's blessings.

3. **Discernment Journal:** Reflect on situations where you need guidance on standing or retreating. Write out what you sense God saying.

Discussion Questions

- What does it mean practically to "bind" and "loose" in your daily life?

- How can believers grow in confidence to use their spiritual authority?

- What are some examples of battles where standing firm or strategic withdrawal altered the outcome?

Prayer Guide

- **Prayer for Boldness:**
  "Lord, help me to walk boldly in the authority You have given me.
  May I use it to bring Your Kingdom on earth."

- **Prayer for Discernment:**
  "Holy Spirit, guide me when to stand firm and when to step back.
  Teach me wisdom in every battle."

- **Prayer for Alignment:** "Father, help me align my will with
  Yours, so my prayers and authority reflect Your perfect plan."

- **Prayer for Authority:**
  "Jesus, thank You for giving me authority over the enemy. Help me
  to walk boldly and confidently in that authority."

Topics Covered

- Delegated authority through Christ

- How to use spiritual authority in prayer and warfare

- Binding and loosing

- When to stand and when to flee

Chapter 5:
The Armor of God

Key Scriptures

- *Ephesians 6:11—"Put on the whole armor of God, that you may be able to stand against the wiles of the devil."*

- *Ephesians 6:13–17*—Describes each piece of the spiritual armor

Overview

God provides us with spiritual armor to protect and enable us to stand firm against the enemy's attacks. The apostle Paul describes the believer's spiritual armor in Ephesians 6:10–18. Each piece has a strategic role in defending and empowering Christians during spiritual battles. The armor of God prepares believers for daily victory. Every piece represents a truth or discipline crucial for remaining steadfast in spiritual warfare.

Expanded Study

1. Belt of Truth

Truth is foundational. The belt secured the Roman soldier's tunic and held the sword. Spiritually, it holds everything together. Truth combats lies and deception.

- **John 8:32**—*"Then you will know the truth, and the truth will set you free."*

- **Psalm 119:160**—*"The sum of Your word is truth."*

Practical Insight: Anchor your life in God's truth, not opinions or feelings. Memorize Scripture to combat the lies of the enemy.

2. Breastplate of Righteousness

The breastplate protected vital organs, especially the heart. Righteousness shields us from condemnation and accusations.

- **2 Corinthians 5:21**—"We are the righteousness of God in Christ."

- **Romans 8:1**—"There is no condemnation for those who are in Christ Jesus."

Practical Insight: Daily remind yourself that you are made righteous through Christ, not by your performance.

3. Shoes of the Gospel of Peace

Roman sandals had spikes for traction and stability. The Gospel brings peace with God and equips us to move forward without fear.

- **Romans 5:1**—"We have peace with God through our Lord Jesus Christ."

- **Isaiah 52:7**—"How beautiful are the feet of those who bring good news."

Practical Insight: Stay grounded in the peace of God. Be ready to share the good news wherever you go.

4. Shield of Faith

The Roman shield covered the entire body and could extinguish flaming arrows. Faith quenches the enemy's attacks—doubt, fear, lies.

- **Hebrews 11:6**—"Without faith it is impossible to please God."

- **1 John 5:4**—"This is the victory that overcomes the world—our faith."

Practical Insight: Speak God's promises aloud. Build your faith by reading testimonies and declaring truth.

5. Helmet of Salvation

The helmet protected the mind. Salvation guards our thoughts with assurance of who we are and where we are going.

- **1 Thessalonians 5:8**—*"...as a helmet, the hope of salvation."*

- **Romans 12:2**—*"Be transformed by the renewing of your mind."*

Practical Insight: Battle negative thoughts by affirming your salvation and God's truth over your life.

6. Sword of the Spirit

The sword is the Word of God—both defensive and offensive. Jesus used it to defeat Satan in the wilderness.

- **Hebrews 4:12**—*"The word of God is living and active, sharper than any two-edged sword."*

- **Matthew 4:4**—*"It is written..."*

Practical Insight: Use Scripture when you pray and when you're under attack. Let the Word be your weapon.

Advanced Exploration

1. Belt of Truth—Living Anchored in God's Word

- The belt was the first piece a Roman soldier put on—it held the rest of the armor in place. Without truth, everything else falls apart.

- **Spiritual Lesson:** Truth is more than facts—it's God's reality. Jesus said, *"I am the way, the truth, and the life"* (John 14:6). To put on the belt means living in alignment with God's Word and Christ Himself.

- The enemy's primary weapon is lies. Lies about God, about you, and about your circumstances. The belt keeps you from falling for deception.

- **Application:** Commit to daily Bible reading and memorization. Let God's truth be your filter for news, culture, and even your own emotions.

---

2. Breastplate of Righteousness—Walking in Holiness

- A Roman breastplate covered the heart and lungs—vital for survival. Spiritually, righteousness protects the heart (the center of desires, thoughts, and will).

- **Two aspects of righteousness:**

  - *Imputed righteousness:* The righteousness of Christ given to us at salvation (Romans 5:17).

  - *Practical righteousness:* Our choices to live holy lives that please God (1 Peter 1:15).

- Satan attacks with guilt and condemnation, trying to pierce the heart. The breastplate protects by reminding us that Christ's righteousness covers us.

- **Application:** When guilt strikes, remember Romans 8:1: *"There is therefore now no condemnation for those who are in Christ Jesus."* Choose daily holiness as a lifestyle of protection.

3. Shoes of Peace—Readiness Through the Gospel

- Soldiers wore studded sandals to give stability and readiness to march long distances. Without proper shoes, they couldn't advance or stand firm.

- Peace comes in two ways:

    - *Peace with God* (Romans 5:1)—no longer enemies of God because of Christ.

    - *Peace of God* (Philippians 4:7)—calmness in trials.

- The Gospel gives both. It makes us ready to share good news and to stand firmly when storms hit.

- **Application:** Stand on peace when conflict arises. When fear tries to destabilize you, pray Philippians 4:6–7. Keep the Gospel on your lips—be ready to encourage others with the hope of Christ.

4. Shield of Faith—Blocking Fiery Darts of Doubt

- Roman shields were tall, door-sized, and often interlocked with others for defense in battle.

- Fiery darts represent sudden attacks: fear, discouragement, temptation, doubt. Faith blocks and extinguishes them.

- Faith is not blind positivity; it's trust in the proven faithfulness of God.

- **Application:** Keep your shield soaked in the Word (Romans 10:17). When fear arises, raise faith by speaking promises aloud. Link shields with other believers—corporate faith in prayer is powerful.

5. Helmet of Salvation—Guarding the Mind

- Helmets protected the soldier from fatal head wounds. Spiritually, salvation guards our minds from lies and hopelessness.

- Satan's most common battlefield is the mind—planting thoughts of fear, confusion, doubt, or condemnation.

- **Salvation provides:**

  - Assurance (John 10:28)

  - Hope of eternal life (Titus 1:2)

  - Renewal of the mind (Romans 12:2)

- **Application:** Declare daily who you are in Christ. When negative thoughts attack, reject them and replace them with Scripture. Example: When you hear "You're not forgiven," answer with 1 John 1:9.

6. Sword of the Spirit—Speaking God's Word

- The sword was the only offensive weapon listed. It could cut in any direction.

- God's Word is described as a sword in Hebrews 4:12—living, active, sharp.

- Jesus modeled sword use when He defeated Satan's temptations by quoting Scripture (Matthew 4).

- **Application:** Memorize specific verses for areas of struggle (fear, temptation, discouragement). Speak them aloud in prayer and warfare. The Word becomes a sword only when spoken, not just when stored in the mind.

How the Armor Works Together

- The armor is not optional; it's a full set for every believer.

- Truth holds everything together.

- Righteousness protects the heart.

- Peace stabilizes and readies us.

- Faith blocks attacks.

- Salvation guards the mind.

- The Word defeats the enemy.

- **Application:** Pray daily to "put on" the full armor (Ephesians 6:11). Visualize each piece as you commit to truth, righteousness, peace, faith, salvation, and the Word.

Common Signs

- Feeling spiritually unprepared

- Easily shaken by trials

- Struggling with doubt or confusion

- Neglecting daily devotion

Example

A student prayed each day through the armor of God before school. This discipline gave him the boldness to resist peer pressure and share his faith.

Biblical Example

Jesus resisted Satan in the wilderness with Scripture—the **Sword of the Spirit**—showing the effectiveness of God's Word in battle.

Practical Insight

Putting on the armor is not mystical but practical—choosing daily to live in truth, faith, righteousness, and the Word.

Key Memory Verses

- Ephesians 6:11–17

- Hebrews 4:12

- Romans 12:2

Reflection Questions

- Which piece of the armor do you feel strongest in?

....

....

....

....

- How can you "put on" the armor daily?

....

....

....

....

- How have you seen the armor protect you in spiritual battles?

....

....

....

....

- Which piece of the armor do you most need to strengthen in your daily life?

....

....

....

....

- How can you put it on intentionally today?

....

....

....

....

....

....

- Which piece of the armor do you need to strengthen today?

....

....

....

....

Exercises

1. **Armor Prayer:** Pray through each piece of the armor every morning, asking God to clothe you in strength and protection.

2. **Scripture Sword Practice:** Memorize and declare Scripture that counters common attacks you face.

3. **Faith Shield:** Write down moments when your faith has protected you. Reflect on those victories when doubt or fear arise.

Discussion Questions

- How do the different pieces of armor work together in spiritual warfare?

- Share testimonies of how using the armor helped you resist temptation or attack.

- What daily habits can help you consistently put on the armor?

Prayer Guide

- **Prayer for Protection:**
  "Lord, clothe me daily in Your armor. Protect my mind, heart, and spirit against the enemy's attacks."

- **Prayer for Faith:**
  "Increase my faith, Father, so I can stand firm and extinguish all fiery darts."

- **Prayer for the Word:**
  "Help me wield Your Word as a powerful weapon to defeat lies and deception."

Daily Prayer: Putting on the Armor of God

(Based on Ephesians 6:10–18)

1. The Belt of Truth

Lord, I put on the belt of truth. Help me to walk in honesty and integrity to-day. Anchor me in Your Word, and let Your truth expose and destroy every lie of the enemy. Jesus, You are the Truth, and I choose to stand on You.

2. The Breastplate of Righteousness

Father, I thank You for the righteousness of Christ that covers me. Guard my heart from condemnation, guilt, and shame. Empower me to walk in holiness and obedience today, making choices that please You and reflect Your character.

3. The Shoes of Peace

Lord, I put on the shoes of the Gospel of peace. Thank You for giving me peace with You and the peace of God in every circumstance. Keep me steady when chaos comes, and make me ready to share the good news of Christ with others today.

4. The Shield of Faith

Father, I lift up the shield of faith. Strengthen my trust in You. Extinguish every fiery dart of fear, doubt, temptation, or discouragement that the enemy launches at me. Help me to stand firm, believing that You are faithful and true.

5. The Helmet of Salvation

Lord, I put on the helmet of salvation. Guard my mind from lies, confusion, and despair. Renew my thoughts with Your Word. Remind me that I am saved, forgiven, and secure in Christ. Fill me with the hope of eternal life.

6. The Sword of the Spirit

Holy Spirit, I take up the sword of the Spirit, which is the Word of God. Bring Your Word to my remembrance when I am under attack. Teach me to declare Scripture with boldness, just as Jesus did. Let Your Word cut down lies and bring victory today.

Closing Prayer

Lord, I thank You that in Christ I am fully armed and fully victorious. I choose to stand strong in Your power and not my own. Cover me with Your presence, lead me by Your Spirit, and use me today as a soldier of light. In Jesus's name, Amen.

Topics Covered

- The reality of spiritual warfare and why armor is essential (Ephesians 6:10–18).

- The Belt of Truth: standing firm against lies and deception.

- The Breastplate of Righteousness: guarding the heart through holiness and Christ's righteousness.

- The Shoes of Peace: finding stability in God's peace and readiness to share the Gospel.

- The Shield of Faith: extinguishing fiery darts of fear, doubt, and temptation.

- The Helmet of Salvation: protecting the mind with assurance, hope, and renewal.

- The Sword of the Spirit: using God's Word as both defense and offense.

- How the armor works together as a complete system of protection and power.

- Practical ways to "put on" the armor daily through prayer, obedience, and Scripture.

- Jesus as the model of wearing and wielding spiritual armor.

- Living as a fully armed believer: advancing God's Kingdom with confidence and victory.

Chapter 6:
The Word of God

Key Scriptures

- *Hebrews 4:12—"For the word of God is living and powerful, and sharper than any two-edged sword."*

- *Matthew 4:4—"It is written: 'Man shall not live by bread alone, but by every word that proceeds from the mouth of God.'"*

Overview

The Word of God is the believer's most powerful tool. It reveals truth, fortifies faith, and dispels lies. By speaking Scripture aloud, we assert our spiritual authority. As our offensive weapon, the Word of God equips us to counter the enemy's tactics. Scripture is essential for triumphing in spiritual warfare.

Expanded Study

1. How Jesus Used the Word in the Wilderness

In Matthew 4:1–11, Jesus responded to each of Satan's temptations with the phrase, *"It is written..."*

- When tempted to turn stones into bread, He quoted Deuteronomy 8:3.

- When tempted to test God, He quoted Deuteronomy 6:16.

- When tempted to worship Satan, He quoted Deuteronomy 6:13.

Practical Insight: Jesus did not reason with the devil; He quoted the Word. This teaches us that Scripture is our ultimate authority and first line of defense.

2. Memorizing and Meditating on Scripture

Memorizing Scripture equips us to respond immediately when spiritual attack comes. Meditation helps the Word move from our minds to our hearts.

- **Psalm 119:11**—*"I have hidden Your word in my heart, that I might not sin against You."*

- **Joshua 1:8**—*"Meditate on it day and night... then you will prosper and succeed."*

Tips for Memorizing

- Write verses on index cards.

- Repeat them during prayer walks.

- Share them with others to reinforce retention.

Tips for Meditating

- Choose a verse and reflect on each word or phrase.

- Ask God to reveal how it applies to your current situation.

3. Speaking the Word in Faith

Declaring Scripture strengthens your faith and enforces spiritual authority.

- **Romans 10:17**—*"Faith comes by hearing, and hearing by the word of God."*

- **Proverbs 18:21**—*"Death and life are in the power of the tongue."*

Practical Insight

- Begin your day by declaring key Scriptures over your life.

- Speak promises of God during challenges instead of fears or doubts.

- Create a "faith confession" list and say it aloud daily.

Advanced Exploration

1. The Word Is Alive and Active (John 1:1; Hebrews 4:12)

- **John 1:1** says: *"In the beginning was the Word, and the Word was with God, and the Word was God."* The Word is not just text; it is a living revelation of God Himself, embodied in Christ.

- **Hebrews 4:12** adds: *"For the word of God is alive and active. Sharper than any double-edged sword, it penetrates even to dividing soul and spirit, joints and marrow; it judges the thoughts and attitudes of the heart."*

- Unlike human words that fade, God's Word carries divine life and creative power (Genesis 1:3). It transforms hearts, convicts of sin, and releases truth.

- **Practical Insight:** When you read the Bible, approach it not as mere information but as God speaking directly to you. Pray: *"Lord, let Your Word come alive in me today."*

2. The Word Renews the Mind (Romans 12:2)

- **Romans 12:2** teaches: *"Do not conform to the pattern of this world, but be transformed by the renewing of your mind."*

- The mind is the battlefield where Satan often attacks with lies, doubt, and fear. The Word reprograms our thinking to align with God's truth.

- Renewal is not instant. It is a process of replacing old thought patterns with God's promises and commands.

- **Practical Insight:** When anxious thoughts arise, replace them with Philippians 4:6–7. When condemned, declare Romans 8:1. This is how the mind is renewed—by trading lies for truth.

3. The Word Equips for Every Good Work (2 Timothy 3:16–17)

- **2 Timothy 3:16–17** declares: *"All Scripture is God-breathed and is useful for teaching, rebuking, correcting and training in righteousness, so that the servant of God may be thoroughly equipped for every good work."*

- The Word equips us in four dimensions:

    - **Teaching**: Reveals truth and doctrine

    - **Rebuking**: Exposes lies and sin

    - **Correcting**: Restores us when we stray

    - **Training**: Builds character and endurance

- Every spiritual battle, ministry calling, and life assignment requires the equipment of God's Word. Without it, we fight unprepared.

- **Practical Insight:** When preparing for a challenge—whether leading, parenting, ministering, or making decisions—seek Scripture that equips you for that moment.

4. Jesus Modeled the Word's Power in Resisting Temptation (Matthew 4:1–11)

- When tempted in the wilderness, Jesus did not argue, negotiate, or rely on human reasoning. He defeated Satan by declaring, *"It is written."*

- Each temptation—lust of the flesh (bread), pride of life (testing God), lust of the eyes (power/kingdoms)—was countered with Scripture.

- Jesus showed us that the Word is not just for study but for active warfare.

- **Practical Insight:** Keep verses "loaded" like arrows in your heart. When temptation comes, don't just think Scripture; **speak it out loud.** The spoken Word is a sword that pushes back darkness.

Common Signs

- Struggling to discern truth from lies

- Weak faith from a lack of Scripture intake

- Difficulty resisting temptation

Example

A woman battling discouragement carried index cards with verses of hope. Speaking them aloud shifted her mindset and strengthened her faith.

Biblical Example

Jesus used Scripture to resist the devil in Matthew 4. He showed the authority and power of God's Word when spoken.

Key Memory Verses

- Matthew 4:4

- Psalm 119:11

- Joshua 1:8

- Romans 10:17

- Isaiah 55:11

Reflection Questions

- How often do you spend time reading or listening to God's Word?

  ....

  ....

  ....

- What verse has encouraged or strengthened you recently?

  ....

  ....

  ....

  ....

  ....

- How can you use Scripture when you feel tempted, afraid, or discouraged?

  ....

  ....

  ....

  ....

  ....

●   Which Bible truth do you need to hold onto more firmly today?

....

....

....

....

●   How can you "speak" the Word like Jesus did to overcome spiritual
    battles?

....

....

....

....

●   What can you do daily to keep God's Word active and alive in
    your heart?

....

....

....

....

....

- Which area of your life needs to be renewed by God's truth right now?

....

....

....

....

....

....

Exercises

1. Identify an area where you feel powerless and write a prayer of declaration.

2. Practice a "binding and loosing" prayer.

3. Journal about how Jesus used His authority and how you can follow His example.

Discussion Questions

- Why is spiritual authority often unused by believers?

- What's the difference between boldness and arrogance?

- How do you currently use the Word of God in your daily life?

- What verses can you commit to memorize this week to build your defense?

Prayer Guide

- **Prayer of Boldness:** "Jesus, help me walk confidently in the authority You've given me."

- **Prayer of Discernment:** "Holy Spirit, teach me when to stand and when to flee."

Topics Covered

- The Word as living and active (John 1:1; Hebrews 4:12).

- The role of the Word in spiritual warfare.

- How the Word renews the mind and transforms thinking (Romans 12:2).

- Scripture as God-breathed and sufficient for teaching, correction, and training (2 Timothy 3:16–17).

- Jesus's example of resisting temptation through Scripture (Matthew 4:1–11).

- Speaking versus only knowing the Word: why declaration matters.

- Storing the Word in the heart through meditation and memorization (Psalm 119:11).

- The Word as a weapon (Sword of the Spirit) against lies, fear, and temptation.

- Practical methods for studying, applying, and declaring Scripture daily.

- Building a "spiritual arsenal" of key verses for life's battles.

Chapter 7: Prayer and Fasting in Spiritual Warfare

Key Scriptures

- *Matthew 17:21—"However, this kind does not go out except by prayer and fasting."*

Overview

Prayer and fasting are two of the most powerful spiritual tools in a believer's arsenal. By combining prayer and fasting, we align ourselves with God's will, weaken the influence of the flesh, and strengthen our spiritual discernment and authority. Prayer connects us to God's power, while fasting sharpens our focus and cultivates humility. Together, they release spiritual breakthroughs and empower believers to overcome challenges.

Expanded Study

1. Why We Pray and Fast

- **To seek God's presence and guidance** (Jeremiah 29:13; Acts 13:2–3)

- **To humble ourselves before the Lord** (Ezra 8:21)

- **To break strongholds and receive deliverance** (Isaiah 58:6)

- **To gain spiritual clarity and strength** (Mark 9:29)

Prayer is communication with God; fasting is consecration to God. Together, they create a spiritual environment for breakthrough.

Practical Insight: Establish regular times of prayer and consider setting aside days of fasting to draw closer to God and receive specific breakthroughs.

2. Biblical Examples

- **Moses** fasted forty days before receiving the Law (Exodus 34:28).

- **Esther** called for a fast to intercede for her people (Esther 4:16).

- **Jesus** fasted before His public ministry (Matthew 4:2).

- **Daniel** fasted for understanding and a breakthrough (Daniel 10:2–3).

- **The early Church** fasted before appointing leaders (Acts 13:2–3).

Each example highlights how fasting and prayer ushered in divine direction, protection, and power.

Three Personal Testimonies

1. Clarity in a Major Decision

"During a three-day fast, I received clarity about a major life decision I had struggled with for months. God confirmed His direction through Scripture and peace."—Anonymous

- For weeks, this believer had been torn between two career opportunities. Both seemed good, but confusion clouded the heart. During a focused three-day fast, distractions faded and God's Word began to speak clearly.

- One morning, while meditating on Proverbs 3:5–6 (*"Trust in the Lord with all your heart and lean not on your own understanding…"*), a deep peace came.

- Within days, confirmation arrived through a sermon and a conversation with a trusted mentor. The decision that once caused anxiety now brought confidence, showing how prayer and fasting open ears to God's voice.

2. Breakthrough in Family Relationships

"After fasting for a breakthrough in my family, my son, who had been distant, suddenly opened up and asked to come to church again."—Anonymous

- This parent carried a heavy burden: a son who had walked away from faith and grown emotionally distant. Ordinary conversations seemed to hit walls of silence.

- Desperate, the parent committed to fasting for three days, asking God to soften his heart. On the second evening, while praying, the parent felt a strong impression. *"Do not give up—love covers a multitude of sins."*

- The very next week, the son unexpectedly sat down and shared his struggles. He admitted feeling lost and asked if he could attend church again. That fast became the doorway for reconciliation and the first step in his return to Christ.

3. Freedom from Fear and Anxiety

"Through consistent prayer and fasting, I experienced freedom from fear and anxiety that had gripped me for years."—Dr. Rosemica D. Bonhomme

- For years, anxiety had been an unseen enemy, producing sleepless nights, racing thoughts, and paralyzing fear. Even simple tasks often felt overwhelming.

- Instead of surrendering to despair, fasting was added to daily prayer. Days of setting aside meals to dwell on Scriptures like Philippians 4:6–7 (*"Do not be anxious about anything..."*) and Psalm 27:1 (*"The Lord is my light and my salvation—whom shall I fear?"*) brought gradual change.

- Breakthrough didn't happen overnight—but over time, a supernatural calm replaced the fear. The weight that once pressed down was lifted. This testimony reveals that prayer and fasting not only break outward chains but also heal inner battles of the heart and mind.

Practical Insight: Keep a journal of prayer and fasting goals, insights received, and answered prayers. It builds faith and helps track spiritual growth.

Advanced Exploration

1. Prayer Is the Believer's Lifeline in Warfare

- **Scripture:** *"Pray in the Spirit on all occasions with all kinds of prayers and requests"* (Ephesians 6:18).

- Prayer is not optional; it is the weapon that activates the armor of God.

- Through prayer, believers invite heaven's authority into earthly situations.

- Prayer aligns us with God's will (Matthew 6:10). It shifts battles from the natural to the supernatural.

- **Practical Insight:** Just as soldiers never enter battle without communication, Christians must stay in constant contact with their Commander. Prayer keeps us sensitive to God's strategies and warnings.

2. Types of Prayer in Warfare

- **Intercessory Prayer**: Standing in the gap for others (Ezekiel 22:30).

- **Petition Prayer**: Asking God for specific needs (Philippians 4:6).

- **Spiritual Warfare Prayer**: Resisting and rebuking demonic attacks (Luke 10:19).

- **Thanksgiving and Praise**: Shifts the atmosphere and silences the enemy (Psalm 149:6–9).

- **Praying in the Spirit (Tongues)**: Builds up the believer and releases mysteries in prayer (1 Corinthians 14:2; Jude 1:20).

- **Practical Insight:** A strong prayer life blends these forms. Warfare is not just rebuking demons but also cultivating intimacy with God.

3. The Role of Fasting in Spiritual Warfare

- **Scripture:** *"This kind does not go out except by prayer and fasting"* (Matthew 17:21).

- Fasting humbles the flesh and sharpens spiritual sensitivity (Ezra 8:23).

- It breaks strongholds, loosens chains, and brings deliverance (Isaiah 58:6).

- Fasting is not hunger-striking to manipulate God; it's surrendering to draw closer to Him.

- **Practical Insight:** Fasting weakens the grip of distraction, sin, or addiction. It declutters the heart, making room for God's power and guidance.

4. Biblical Examples of Prayer and Fasting in Warfare

- **Daniel (Daniel 10:2–14):** His twenty-one-day fast brought angelic breakthrough in a spiritual battle.

- **Esther (Esther 4:16):** A three-day fast turned national destruction into deliverance.

- **Jesus (Matthew 4:1–11):** His forty-day fast prepared Him to resist Satan's temptations and launch His ministry.

- **Early Church (Acts 13:2–3):** Prayer and fasting preceded major assignments and missionary breakthroughs.

- **Practical Insight:** These examples reveal that fasting is not just personal discipline but a weapon for breakthrough in families, churches, and nations.

5. Power Released Through Prayer and Fasting

- Brings clarity and spiritual direction (Acts 14:23).

- Strengthens authority over demonic forces (Luke 10:19).

- Breaks patterns of fear, addiction, and oppression (Isaiah 58:6–8).

- Unlocks divine provision and protection (Ezra 8:23).

- Cultivates intimacy with God and spiritual empowerment (Matthew 6:17–18).

- **Practical Insight:** Fasting intensifies prayer. Think of prayer as fire and fasting as gasoline—together they ignite greater power in warfare.

6. Practical Guidelines for Fasting in Warfare

- **Set Purpose:** Enter with clear goals (deliverance, healing, direction, intimacy).

- **Start Small:** If new, begin with partial fasts (like Daniel's fast) before longer ones.

- **Stay in the Word:** Replace meals with Scripture, prayer, and worship.

- **Guard Your Heart:** Fasting without humility and prayer is just dieting (Matthew 6:16–18).

- **End Wisely:** Break fasts gradually and with thanksgiving.

- **Practical Insight:** A fast disconnected from prayer is powerless. Always pair fasting with intentional time in God's presence.

Common Signs

- Feeling spiritually stagnant

- Prayers that feel powerless

- Struggling with strongholds or addictions

Example

A church fasted for three days seeking a breakthrough. Afterward, revival broke out, and many came to Christ.

Biblical Example

Esther and her people fasted before she went to the king. God used her courage to save Israel from destruction (Esther 4:16).

Practical Insight

Fasting is not about earning favor but about removing distractions to focus on God.

Key Memory Verses

- Matthew 6:17–18

- Isaiah 58:6

- Jeremiah 29:13

- Acts 13:2–3

Reflection Questions

- What breakthrough are you currently seeking?

- How can you engage in prayer and fasting to draw closer to God and receive His wisdom and power?

....

....

....

....

- Plan a time of focused prayer or fasting this week. What are you believing God to do?

....

....

....

....

Exercises

1. **Plan a Fast**: Choose a method of fasting (full, partial, Daniel fast, etc.) and commit to one to three days. Write your focus and prayer points.

2. **Prayer Journal**: Record what the Holy Spirit reveals each day of your fast.

3. **Scripture Reflection**: Meditate on Isaiah 58 and reflect on the kind of fast that pleases God.

Discussion Questions

- How has fasting impacted your spiritual life in the past?

- Why do you think prayer becomes more powerful when combined with fasting?

- How can you incorporate fasting regularly into your walk with God?

Prayer Guide

- **Prayer of Consecration and Spiritual Breakthrough**: "Heavenly Father, as I humble myself through fasting and prayer, draw me closer to You. Align my heart with Your will, break every stronghold, and release Your power in my life. In Jesus's name, Amen."

Topics Covered

- The biblical foundation of prayer and fasting (Matthew 6:16–18; Acts 13:2–3).

- Why fasting intensifies prayer and sharpens spiritual sensitivity.

- How prayer and fasting break spiritual strongholds (Isaiah 58:6).

- Jesus as the model: fasting before beginning His ministry (Matthew 4:1–11).

- Old Testament examples of breakthrough through fasting (Esther 4:16; Daniel 9:3).

- Personal and corporate fasting: when individuals and churches fast together.

- The role of fasting in discernment, guidance, and decision-making.

- Fasting as a tool for humility, surrender, and dependence on God.

- Overcoming spiritual oppression, fear, and temptation through fasting.

- Practical ways to prepare for and practice prayer and fasting safely.

- Modern testimonies of breakthrough through prayer and fasting.

- Integrating prayer and fasting into a lifestyle, not just a one-time event.

Chapter 8:
The Role of Worship

Key Scriptures

- *2 Chronicles 20:22—"As they began to sing and praise, the Lord set ambushes against the men of Ammon and Moab and Mount Seir who were invading Judah, and they were defeated."*

- *2 Chronicles 20—Jehoshaphat's worship team led the army to victory.*

Overview

Worship shifts the atmosphere and invites God's presence into battle. Worship is more than music; it is a powerful weapon in spiritual warfare. When we praise God in the face of adversity, we proclaim His greatness above our circumstances. Worship invites God's presence, confuses the enemy, and strengthens our spirit.

Expanded Study

1. Worship as Warfare

Worship aligns our hearts with heaven and invites God's presence into our battles. It reminds us who God is and who we are in Him.

- **Psalm 22:3**—God inhabits the praises of His people.

- **Acts 16:25–26**—Paul and Silas worshiped in prison, and God released a miracle.

Practical Insight: When you're under attack, worship as an act of defiance against fear and discouragement. Worship shifts the spiritual atmosphere.

2. Praise in the Storm

Praising God amid trials demonstrates trust and releases divine intervention. King Jehoshaphat's army worshiped ahead of battle, and God fought for them.

- **Habakkuk 3:17–18**—Even when there's no fruit or harvest, yet will I rejoice in the Lord.

- **Job 1:20–21**—After great loss, Job worshiped.

Practical Insight: Make a habit of worshiping God *before* you see the victory. Praise is a declaration of faith.

3. The Power of Music and Declarations

Music stirs the spirit and helps engage the heart. Declarations made through songs or spoken words carry spiritual authority.

- **1 Samuel 16:23**—David's music drove away tormenting spirits.

- **Psalm 149:6–9**—Let high praises be in their mouth...to bind kings with chains.

Practical Insight

- Build a playlist of anointed worship songs.

- Sing Scripture aloud.

- Declare God's promises daily to stir your faith.

Worship in Spiritual Warfare

1. Worship Focuses Hearts on God, Not Problems (Psalm 22:3)

- **Biblical Insight:** Psalm 22:3 declares that God *"inhabits the praises of His people."* When believers choose to worship, their perspective shifts away from the weight of their struggles and toward the greatness of God.

- **Practical Application:** Problems may not disappear instantly, but worship lifts the heart into God's presence, where peace and strength are found. For example, when bills pile up or sickness weighs heavy, singing songs of adoration redirects attention. *"Lord, You are my Provider. You are my Healer."*

- **Connection to Warfare:** The enemy wants believers trapped in fear and self-focus. Worship is an act of defiance; it declares that God is bigger than the battle.

---

2. Worship Brings Freedom (Acts 16:25–26)

- **Biblical Insight:** Paul and Silas, beaten and imprisoned, chose to sing hymns at midnight. As they worshiped, God shook the prison, opened the doors, and loosed their chains. Their worship literally brought deliverance.

- **Practical Application:** Worship has the power to break inner chains too—fear, depression, or despair. Singing or praying out loud when the heart feels bound is not natural, but it aligns the believer with heaven's power.

- **Connection to Warfare:** Where worship rises, strongholds crumble. Demons flee in the presence of praise, because worship invites God's authority into the situation.

---

3. Worship Confuses the Enemy and Opens Doors to Victory

- **Biblical Insight:** In 2 Chronicles 20:21–22, King Jehoshaphat sent singers ahead of the army to praise God. As they worshiped, the Lord caused their enemies to turn on each other. The battle was won through worship, not weapons.

- **Practical Application:** When believers worship in the face of attacks—whether sickness, opposition, or fear—the enemy is thrown into confusion. He expects despair, not praise. Worship declares that victory belongs to the Lord, even before the outcome is visible.

- **Connection to Warfare:** Worship is not a passive act; it is a spiritual weapon. By lifting praise, believers partner with God, and His power goes forth to fight battles unseen.

Common Signs

- Atmosphere of heaviness or fear

- Difficulty praying or focusing

- Emotional oppression

Example

A woman struggling with anxiety began filling her home with worship music. Over time, fear lifted, and peace filled her heart.

Biblical Example

Paul and Silas worshiped in prison. God shook the foundations, opened doors, and set them free (Acts 16).

Practical Insight

Worship is a weapon—it magnifies God and minimizes fear.

Key Memory Verses

- 2 Chronicles 20:22

- Psalm 22:3

- Habakkuk 3:17–18

- Psalm 149:6–9

Reflection Questions

- What role does worship currently play in your spiritual life?

....

....

....

....

....

- How can you use praise as a regular part of your warfare strategy?

....

....

....

....

- Make worship part of your battle plan.

- Sing or play a worship song, and invite God's presence.

- Praise is an act of defiance against fear, doubt, and despair.

- Worship realigns our perspective to God's greatness, not our problems.

- Praise focuses on who God is rather than what we feel.

Exercises

1. **Worship Battle Plan**: Create a three-day worship plan where you intentionally start each day with fifteen minutes of praise.

2. **Write a Declaration**: Craft a personal praise declaration using Scripture, declaring who God is in your situation.

3. **Testify Through Song**: Choose one worship song, and write how it connects to your spiritual battle.

Discussion Questions

- How has worship changed your spiritual environment during a storm?

- Why does praise affect the atmosphere around us?

- What role does music play in your personal spiritual life?

- How does worship affect your spiritual battles?

- Have you ever experienced a breakthrough that came through worship? If so, can you share it?

Prayer Guide

- **Prayer of Praise & Surrender:** "Father, I praise You not only in the good times, but even in the midst of the storm. Let my worship be a weapon. Let praise rise up in my spirit and shift the atmosphere. I trust You, and I exalt You above every enemy. In Jesus's name, Amen."

- **Prayer of Worship & Spiritual Warfare:** "Lord, let my worship be a sweet aroma that defeats the enemy and invites Your power."

Topics Covered

- Worship as warfare

- Praise in the storm

- The power of music and declarations

Chapter 9:
The Name and Blood of Jesus

Key Scriptures

- *Philippians 2:10—"That at the name of Jesus every knee should bow, in heaven and on earth and under the earth."*

- *Revelation 12:11—"They overcame him by the blood of the Lamb and by the word of their testimony."*

Overview

The name and blood of Jesus hold immense power to break every chain and dispel darkness. Jesus's victory over sin, death, and the devil is absolute and complete. As believers, we triumph by understanding the authority of Jesus's name, applying the power of His blood, and embracing the reality of His finished work on the cross. The name of Jesus carries authority, commanding respect and obedience, while His blood covers, protects, and redeems, providing forgiveness and cleansing. By faithfully relying on these spiritual realities, we can walk in victory, overcoming challenges and living a life that reflects the triumph of Christ.

Expanded Study

1. The Authority of Jesus's Name

Jesus's name carries absolute authority in heaven and on earth. When believers speak His name in faith, it represents His presence, power, and victory.

- **Acts 3:6**—Peter healed the lame man *"in the name of Jesus Christ of Nazareth."*

- **John 14:13–14**—*"Whatever you ask in My name, I will do..."*

Practical Insight

- When confronting darkness, speak boldly in Jesus's name.

- Pray with authority. "In Jesus's name, I command fear to go."

2. Pleading the Blood of Jesus

The blood of Jesus is a powerful spiritual weapon. It represents redemption, forgiveness, and protection. Pleading the blood is declaring the covering and cleansing power of Christ over situations.

- **Exodus 12:13**—The blood on the doorposts caused the destroyer to pass over.

- **Hebrews 9:14**—The blood of Christ cleanses our conscience.

Practical Insight

- Plead the blood in prayer over your home, family, and mind.

- Say aloud, "I plead the blood of Jesus over my thoughts, my children, and my future."

3. Applying His Finished Work in Spiritual Battles

Jesus declared, *"It is finished"* on the cross (John 19:30), meaning every debt was paid, and every victory secured. We fight not for victory, but from victory.

- **Colossians 2:15**—*Jesus disarmed the powers and authorities.*

- **Romans 8:37**—*"We are more than conquerors through Him who loved us."*

The Power of the Name and Blood of Jesus

1. The Name of Jesus Represents His Authority (Philippians 2:9–10)

- **Biblical Insight:** Philippians 2:9–10 tells us that God exalted Jesus and gave Him *"the name that is above every name, that at the name of Jesus every knee should bow, in heaven and on earth* *and under the earth.*" His name is not just a title; it carries divine authority and power over all realms.

- **Spiritual Application:** When believers pray "in Jesus's name," they are not reciting a formula but invoking the authority of the risen Christ. Demons tremble at His name (Luke 10:17), healing is released in His name (Acts 3:6), and prayers are answered through His name (John 14:13–14).

- **Warfare Connection:** In spiritual conflict, calling on the name of Jesus asserts His lordship over fear, sickness, oppression, or demonic activity. It is a direct declaration that the battle belongs to Him.

2. His Blood Redeems, Cleanses, and Protects (Hebrews 9:14)

- **Biblical Insight:** Hebrews 9:14 teaches that the blood of Christ cleanses our conscience from dead works so we may serve the living God. The blood represents Christ's sacrifice on the cross, which accomplished redemption, forgiveness, and victory over sin and death.

- **Spiritual Application:** The blood is not only about salvation; it is also about ongoing cleansing (1 John 1:7) and spiritual covering. Just as the Israelites applied the blood of the lamb to their doorposts at Passover (Exodus 12:13), believers can declare the power of Christ's blood as protection over their lives, families, and homes.

- **Warfare Connection:** The enemy is disarmed through the blood because it testifies that his accusations no longer stand (Revelation 12:11). Speaking the truth of the blood reminds Satan that he is already defeated.

3. Believers Overcome by Declaring His Finished Work

- **Biblical Insight:** Revelation 12:11 says, *"They overcame him by the blood of the Lamb and by the word of their testimony."* Victory in warfare is tied to both what Christ has done (the blood) and what believers declare (their testimony).

- **Spiritual Application:** Overcoming involves speaking truth aloud: "I am redeemed by the blood. I am forgiven. I am free." These declarations align the believer with God's reality and silence the enemy's lies. Faith grows stronger when words of victory replace words of defeat.

- **Warfare Connection:** The finished work of Jesus—His death, resurrection, and exaltation—means the enemy's power is broken. Declaring it out loud is not for God's reminder but for the believer's strengthening and the enemy's rebuke.

Common Signs

- Nightmares or fear in sleep

- Struggles with guilt and condemnation

- Feelings of vulnerability

Example

A believer plagued with nightmares prayed, "I plead the blood of Jesus over my mind and sleep." Peace came, and the nightmares stopped.

Biblical Example

Peter healed a lame man by declaring: *"In the name of Jesus Christ of Nazareth, rise up and walk" (Acts 3:6).*

Practical Insight

- When under attack, declare Christ's finished work: "I am forgiven, redeemed, and victorious through Jesus."

- Stand on Scripture and refuse to accept defeat as your portion.

- The blood of Jesus is not symbolic only. It has real spiritual power when applied by faith.

Key Memory Verses

- Philippians 2:10

- Revelation 12:11

- John 19:30

- Colossians 2:15

Reflection Questions

- Are you walking in the full authority Jesus gave you? How can you use His name, His blood, and His finished work in your daily spiritual battles?

- How can you declare the name of Jesus over your situation today?

- In what ways does the name of Jesus carry the weight of heaven's authority in your life?

- How do you understand the truth that the blood of Jesus is not a magical formula but a spiritual reality we embrace by faith?

....

....

....

....

....

When we operate from Christ's finished work, we are not trying to win; we are enforcing a victory already secured.

Exercises

1. **Declare the Name**: Make a list of situations in your life and boldly pray over each one in the name of Jesus.

2. **Blood Covering Exercise**: Plead the blood of Jesus over your home, family, and mind each morning for seven days.

3. **Victory Walk**: Write a declaration that affirms your identity and authority in Christ based on His finished work.

Discussion Questions

- Why is Jesus's name more than just a word? What does it represent?

- How do we practically "plead the blood" over areas of our lives?

- What does it mean to live from Christ's finished work instead of striving in our own strength?

Prayer Guide

- **Prayer for Protection and Covering :** Lord Jesus, I honor Your powerful name. I plead Your blood over my life—my mind, my home, and everything You have entrusted to me. Thank You that Your work is finished and that Your victory is mine. Help me to walk boldly in this authority, bringing glory to Your name. Amen.

Prayers and Declarations

1. The Name of Jesus: Authority in Prayer

Prayer:
"Father, I thank You that You have given Jesus the name above every name. In His name, I stand in authority over fear, doubt, and every attack of the enemy. Let every knee bow to the Lordship of Jesus in my life, my family, and my circumstances. Amen."

Declarations

- "In the name of Jesus, fear must bow."

- "In the name of Jesus, sickness must flee."

- "In the name of Jesus, every plan of the enemy is destroyed."

2. The Blood of Jesus: Redemption and Protection

Prayer:
"Lord Jesus, I plead Your blood over my life, my mind, my family, and my home. Thank You that Your blood redeems, cleanses, and protects me. Let every accusation of the enemy be silenced by the power of Your blood."

Declarations

- "By the blood of Jesus, I am redeemed from the power of sin."

- "By the blood of Jesus, my household is covered and protected."

- "By the blood of Jesus, every curse is broken and every chain destroyed."

---

3. Declaring His Finished Work

Prayer:
"Lord, I thank You that on the cross You declared, 'It is finished.' I walk in that victory today. I reject the lies of the enemy and stand in the truth of who I am in You. Strengthen me to declare Your promises boldly."

Declarations

- *"I overcome by the blood of the Lamb and the word of my testimony (Revelation 12:11)."*

- *"I am forgiven, free, and victorious in Christ."*

- *"The enemy is defeated—Jesus reigns forever."*

Summary

- The **name of Jesus** releases divine authority in heaven, on earth, and over darkness.

- The **blood of Jesus** redeems, cleanses, and shields believers.

* The **declaration of His finished work** is how Christians actively walk in victory.

Topics Covered

* The exaltation of Jesus's name above every name (Philippians 2:9–10).

* Authority in spiritual warfare through the name of Jesus (Luke 10:17; Acts 3:6).

* The blood of Jesus as the foundation of redemption and cleansing (Hebrews 9:14; 1 John 1:7).

* The protective power of the blood, echoing the Passover (Exodus 12:13).

* Silencing the enemy's accusations through the blood of the Lamb (Revelation 12:11).

* Declaring the finished work of Christ in daily life and battles.

* How to "plead the blood" biblically and effectively.

* Overcoming fear, guilt, and oppression through Jesus's name and blood.

* The link between testimony, declaration, and victory.

* Practical prayers and declarations for warfare, protection, and breakthrough.

* Living a lifestyle of confidence in Christ's victory.

Chapter 10:
Recognizing Demonic Influence

Key Scriptures

- *2 Corinthians 10:4—"For the weapons of our warfare are not carnal but mighty in God for pulling down strongholds."*

- *Ephesians 6:12—"For we do not wrestle against flesh and blood, but against principalities, against powers..."*

- *2 Corinthians 2:11—"Lest Satan should take advantage of us; for we are not ignorant of his devices."*

Overview

We must be alert to the enemy's influence, but not fearful. Discernment is key. Understanding how the enemy operates helps us discern and overcome his tactics. Not all challenges are demonic in origin, but many spiritual battles are intensified by unseen opposition. Recognizing the signs and roots of demonic oppression and strongholds is crucial in spiritual warfare.

Expanded Study

1. Signs of Demonic Oppression

Demonic oppression refers to external pressure or harassment from demonic spirits. It does not mean someone is possessed but that they are under the influence.

Common Signs

- Unrelenting fear, depression, or hopelessness

- Recurring sinful behavior or addictions despite repentance

- Hearing accusatory, condemning, or blasphemous thoughts

- Constant confusion or difficulty focusing on spiritual matters

- Unexplained illness or chronic fatigue with no medical cause

Example: A woman experiences intense anxiety only when trying to attend church or pray. After prayer and deliverance ministry, the fear lifts, revealing demonic oppression targeting her spiritual life.

---

2. Spiritual Strongholds and Bondage

A stronghold is a mindset or belief system that opposes God's truth and gives the enemy a foothold.

Root Causes of Strongholds

- Trauma or abuse

- Lies believed about oneself or God

- Repetitive sin or generational curses

Biblical Example

- The Israelites feared the giants in Canaan despite God's promises (Numbers 13:33). Their fear became a mental stronghold that delayed their victory.

Practical Insight

- Identify lies you believe (e.g., "I'll never change") and replace them with truth (e.g., "I am a new creation" (2 Corinthians 5:17).

- Daily declare God's truth over your thoughts.

- Surround yourself with spiritually grounded believers who can help you discern and stand firm.

3. Influence in Thoughts, Emotions, and Behavior

The enemy often targets the mind first, planting lies, doubts, or temptations. When these take root, they can influence emotions and lead to destructive behaviors.

Progression of Influence

1. **Thought**: "God doesn't hear my prayers."

2. **Emotion**: Hopelessness or bitterness

3. **Behavior**: Withdrawal from prayer and fellowship

Romans 12:2 calls us to be transformed by renewing our minds with God's Word.

Key Memory Verses

- 2 Corinthians 10:4–5

- Ephesians 6:12

- Romans 12:2

- John 8:32

Reflection Questions

- Have you noticed patterns of spiritual attack in your thoughts or emotions?

....

....

....

- What lies might be at the root of any strongholds in your life?

....

....

....

- How can you ask the Holy Spirit to reveal any areas in your life where darkness may be hiding?

....

....

....

- Why is it important to recognize what we cannot fight, and how does awareness bring the light of God's truth?

- How does the truth that Jesus came to destroy the works of the devil (1 John 3:8) apply to setting the oppressed free today?

- In what ways does the Holy Spirit gently reveal what the enemy tries to keep hidden in your life?

Exercises

1. **Self-Assessment**: Identify any emotional patterns or cycles of behavior that could be linked to oppression or strongholds.

2. **Truth Exchange**: Write out a lie you've believed, and replace it with a Scripture-based truth.

3. **Freedom Journal**: Keep a seven-day journal where you ask the Holy Spirit to show you any areas where freedom is needed.

Discussion Questions

- What are some warning signs of demonic influence in a believer's life?

- How can we identify the difference between natural struggles and spiritual oppression?

- Why is renewing the mind critical in breaking strongholds?

Prayer Guide

- Prayer of Deliverance and Discernment: "Heavenly Father, open my eyes to any area where I've allowed the enemy access. Reveal every stronghold and replace it with Your truth. I receive Your freedom through Jesus Christ and declare that no weapon formed against me will prosper. In Jesus's name, Amen."

Topics Covered

- Signs of demonic oppression

- Spiritual strongholds and bondage

- Influence in thoughts, emotions, and behavior

Chapter 11: Principles of Deliverance

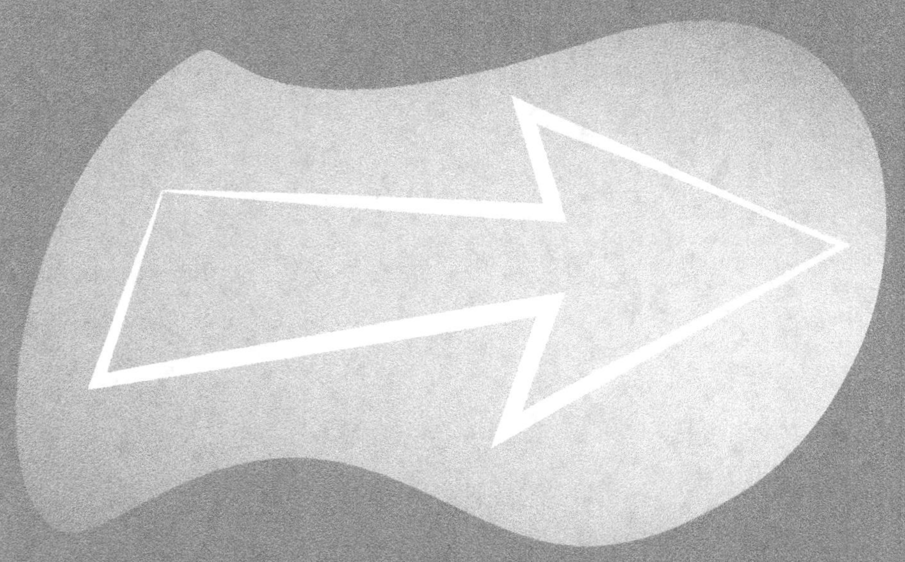

Key Scriptures

- *Luke 4:18—"He has sent Me to proclaim liberty to the captives..."*

- *Mark 16:17—"And these signs will follow those who believe: In My name they will cast out demons..."*

Overview

Deliverance is a ministry of love, freedom, compassion, and restoration. It's about setting captives free through the authority of Jesus. It is the process by which individuals are set free from demonic oppression, bondage, or influence. Jesus regularly cast out demons and has given His Church authority to do the same. This chapter explores biblical examples, signs that someone may need deliverance, common misconceptions, and how to approach deliverance in a safe, Christ-centered way.

Expanded Study

1. Biblical Examples of Deliverance

- **Mark 5:1–20**—The man with a legion of demons in the region of the Gerasenes. After Jesus cast the demons out, the man was found clothed and in his right mind.

- **Luke 13:10–17**—A woman bent over for eighteen years, described as "bound by Satan," was delivered by Jesus in a synagogue.

- **Acts 16:16–18**—Paul cast out a spirit of divination from a slave girl who was being exploited.

Practical Insight: Deliverance was a normal part of Jesus's ministry and continued in the early Church. We must recover it as a compassionate and discerning ministry today.

2. Signs Someone May Need Deliverance

Deliverance is not only for the demon-possessed, but also for the oppressed. Some signs include:

- Persistent tormenting thoughts (especially suicidal or violent)

- Uncontrollable urges, especially with sin (e.g., sexual immorality, rage, substance abuse)

- Unusual body reactions during prayer (screaming, convulsing, etc.)

- Hatred for God, the Bible, or worship without explanation

- Generational patterns of destruction or occult involvement

Example: A man struggling with pornography for years had gone through counseling and prayer, but nothing changed. During a deliverance session, a spirit of lust was discerned and cast out, leading to newfound freedom.

3. Misconceptions About Deliverance

- **Myth: Only non-Christians can have demons.**

  - **Truth:** While Christians cannot be *possessed* (owned), they can be *oppressed* or influenced in mind, body, or emotions.

- **Myth: Deliverance is dramatic or scary.**

  - **Truth:** Some deliverances are quiet and peaceful. Others may be intense but are not to be feared.

- **Myth: Deliverance is a one-time fix.**

  - **Truth:** Deliverance may be instant or progressive. Maintaining freedom requires discipleship, renewing the mind, and staying in community.

4. Basic Steps to Administer or Receive Deliverance

1. **Confession and Repentance**—Acknowledge any sin, unforgiveness, or occult involvement.

   - ○ **1 John 1:9**—*"If we confess our sins, He is faithful and just to forgive..."*

2. **Renunciation**—Verbally reject lies, sins, or occult ties.

   - ○ Example: "I renounce every agreement I made with fear, lust, witchcraft, etc."

3. **Command the Spirits to Leave**—In Jesus's name, not by your own power.

   - ○ Example: "In the name of Jesus, I command every unclean spirit to leave me now."

4. **Fill the Empty Space**—Ask the Holy Spirit to fill every area and invite God's truth to dwell there.

   - ○ **Matthew 12:43–45** warns of unclean spirits returning to an empty house.

5. **Follow-Up and Discipleship**—Connect the person to pastoral care, Bible study, and accountability.

Practical Insight: Deliverance should always be Christ-centered, Spirit-led, and rooted in love—not fear or pride.

Key Memory Verses

- Luke 4:18

- Mark 16:17

- 1 John 1:9

- Matthew 12:43–45

Reflection Questions

- Have you or someone you know shown signs of demonic oppression?

....

....

....

....

....

- What areas of your life might need healing and freedom?

....

....

....

....

....

- Are you open to the Holy Spirit leading you into deeper liberty in Christ?

- Have you or someone you know experienced spiritual bondage, and how can you ask God to guide you into healing and freedom?

- How does understanding that deliverance is an act of love and mercy, rather than fear, change the way you approach it?

- Why is freedom considered a process, and how does deliverance through one encounter continue through discipleship?

....

....

....

....

- In what ways does the truth that Jesus came to destroy every work of the enemy show that your freedom is His will?

....

....

....

....

Exercises

1. **Freedom Reflection**: Journal about any area where you feel bound or tormented. Bring this before God.

2. **Steps of Release**: Write out a repentance and renunciation prayer tailored to your situation.

3. **Freedom Plan**: Create a follow-up plan with Scripture, community, and spiritual disciplines.

Discussion Questions

- What fears or myths have you heard about deliverance?

- What does biblical deliverance look like compared to Hollywood portrayals?

- Why is it important to combine deliverance with discipleship and support?

Prayer Guide

- **Prayer of Deliverance and Spiritual Cleansing**: "Jesus, You came to set me free. I confess any sin, I renounce every agreement with darkness, and I receive Your deliverance. Fill me with Your Holy Spirit. Guard my mind, body, and spirit, and help me walk in truth every day. In Your powerful name I pray, Amen."

Topics Covered

- Biblical examples of deliverance

- Signs someone may need deliverance

- Misconceptions about deliverance

- Basic steps to administer or receive deliverance

Chapter 12:
Walking in Freedom

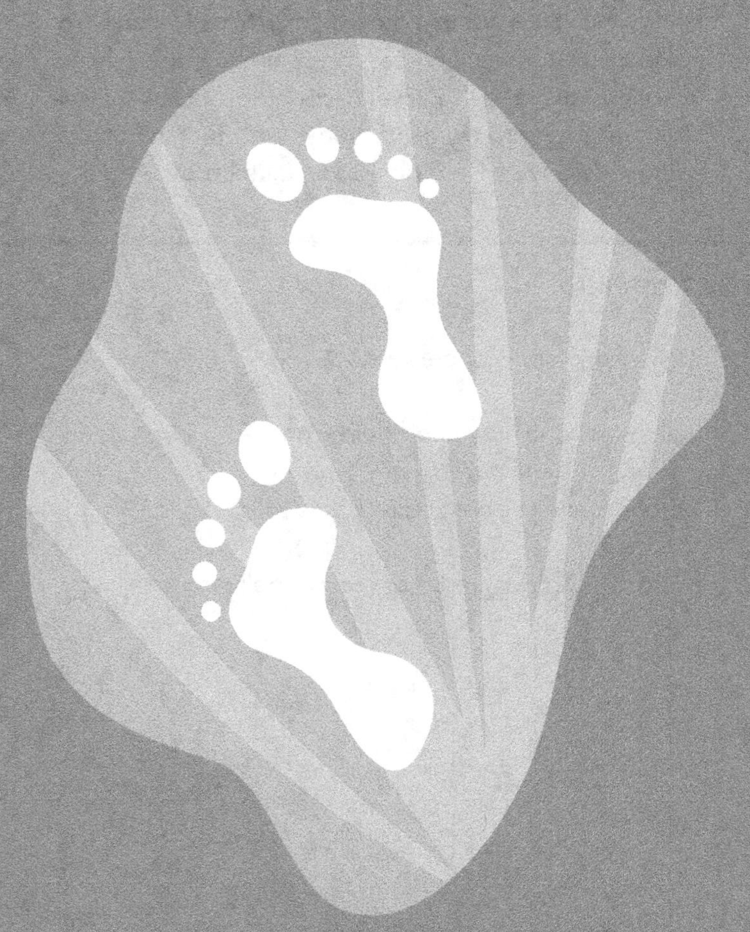

Key Scriptures

- *Galatians 5:1—"It is for freedom that Christ has set us free. Stand firm, then, and do not let yourselves be burdened again by a yoke of slavery."*

- *Romans 12:2—"Do not conform to the pattern of this world, but be transformed by the renewing of your mind."*

Overview

Deliverance is not the end; it's the beginning of a lifestyle of freedom. Walking in freedom means maintaining victory through daily spiritual disciplines. Maintaining freedom requires intentionality. In this chapter, we'll explore how to break cycles of sin and temptation, stay filled with the Holy Spirit, renew the mind, and stay accountable within a godly community.

Expanded Study

1. Breaking Cycles of Sin and Temptation

Cycles of sin often have spiritual, emotional, and habitual roots. Breaking them requires identifying triggers, repentance, spiritual discipline, and replacing lies with truth.

Example: A man who repeatedly returned to alcohol realized his pattern was linked to stress and loneliness. Through prayer, counseling, and replacing isolation with godly friendships, the cycle was broken.

Practical Insight

- Recognize your patterns and their triggers.

- Replace temptation with spiritual discipline—prayer, worship, Scripture.

- Use accountability partners to confess and pray regularly (James 5:16).

2. Staying Filled with the Holy Spirit

Freedom must be filled with God's presence. Being filled with the Holy Spirit empowers you to resist temptation and live victoriously.

- **Ephesians 5:18**—*"Be filled with the Spirit."*

- **Galatians 5:16**—*"Walk by the Spirit, and you will not gratify the desires of the flesh."*

Practical Insight

- Ask the Holy Spirit to fill you daily.

- Practice listening prayer, speaking in tongues (if gifted), and surrender.

3. Renewing the Mind

Freedom begins in the mind. What you think shapes how you live.

- **2 Corinthians 10:5**—*"We take captive every thought to make it obedient to Christ."*

Example: A woman delivered from fear began to declare Scriptures like Psalm 27 and Isaiah 41:10 every morning. Her mindset shifted and fear lost its grip.

Practical Insight

- Meditate on truth daily.

- Journal lies you've believed and write out God's truth in response.

4. Accountability and Community

Isolation is a trap of the enemy. God uses community to protect and grow us.

- **Hebrews 10:24-25**—*"Let us not give up meeting together... but encourage one another."*

Practical Insight

- Join a small group or Bible study.

- Meet regularly with a mature believer for prayer and encouragement.

- Be honest about your struggles in safe spaces.

Key Memory Verses

- Galatians 5:1

- Romans 12:2

- 2 Corinthians 10:5

- Hebrews 10:25

Reflection Questions

- Are there cycles you need to break with the help of the Holy Spirit and trusted believers? How can you actively renew your mind and protect your freedom?

- What steps can you take to preserve your spiritual freedom this week?

- How can daily surrender and intentional habits help maintain your freedom?

Why is isolation dangerous, and how does walking in community support spiritual growth?

In what ways is the mind a battlefield, and how can renewal serve as both a defensive and offensive strategy?

Exercises

1. **Temptation Journal**: Identify areas where you are most tempted. Record patterns and victories.

2. **Mind Renewal Plan**: Choose three Scriptures that speak to your area of struggle and commit to memorizing them.

3. **Accountability Check**: Reach out to a trusted believer and invite regular check-ins for encouragement and support.

Discussion Questions

- What practical steps have helped you overcome sinful patterns?

- How do you stay filled with the Holy Spirit in daily life?

- Why is community essential for spiritual growth and freedom?

Prayer Guide

- **Prayer of Thanksgiving and Spiritual Growth**: "Lord, thank You for setting me free. Help me to walk daily in that freedom, not returning to old ways. Fill me afresh with Your Holy Spirit, renew my mind with truth, and surround me with godly community that builds me up. I choose to live as a new creation in You. In Jesus's name, Amen."

Topics Covered

- Breaking cycles of sin and temptation

- Staying filled with the Holy Spirit

- Renewing the mind

- Accountability and community

Chapter 13:
Cultivating Discernment

Key Scriptures

- *Hebrews 5:14—"But solid food is for the mature, who by constant use have trained themselves to distinguish good from evil."*

- *1 John 4:1—"Dear friends, do not believe every spirit, but test the spirits to see whether they are from God..."*

- *John 16:13—"But when he, the Spirit of truth, comes, he will guide you into all the truth."*

Overview

Spiritual discernment is essential for recognizing what is from God, what is of the flesh, and what is of the enemy. It helps believers distinguish truth from error and walk wisely in a world full of deception. True discernment comes from the Holy Spirit and guards our spiritual atmosphere. In this chapter, we explore how to walk in discernment, not suspicion; rely on the Holy Spirit's guidance; and protect the spiritual atmosphere around us.

Expanded Study

1. Difference Between Suspicion and Discernment

Suspicion is rooted in fear, control, or past wounds; it leads to judgment without evidence. Discernment is spiritual insight given by the Holy Spirit.

Example: A person may feel uneasy around someone and immediately assume wrongdoing. That's suspicion. Discernment, by contrast, may sense something spiritually unhealthy, leading to prayer or gentle inquiry rather than accusation.

Practical Insight

- Ask: Is my reaction based on fear or led by the Spirit?

- True discernment always aligns with love and truth (1 Corinthians 13).

2. The Role of the Holy Spirit

The Holy Spirit is the believer's internal compass. He reveals truth, exposes error, and protects us from deception.

- **John 16:13**—The Spirit guides into all truth.

- **1 Corinthians 2:14**—Spiritual truths are spiritually discerned.

Practical Insight

- Cultivate intimacy with the Holy Spirit through prayer and worship.

- Trust the inner witness and peace (or lack of peace) He provides.

3. Testing the Spirits (1 John 4:1)

Not all supernatural activity is from God. We are called to test spirits.

Tests to Apply

- **Doctrine of Christ**—Does the spirit confess Jesus as Lord and Messiah? (1 John 4:2–3)

- **Fruits of the Spirit**—Is there love, peace, humility, or manipulation, fear, and pride?

- **Scriptural Alignment**—Does the message align with God's Word?

Example: A prophecy may sound accurate but must still be judged by Scripture and fruit.

4. Protecting Your Spiritual Atmosphere

The environment around you affects your spirit. Guard what you allow into your home, mind, and relationships.

Practical Tips

- Evaluate the media, music, and messages you consume.

- Anoint your home with oil and declare it a dwelling place for God.

- Keep worship music and Scripture reading part of your routine.

Example: A family noticed increased tension and nightmares in their home. Upon removing occult books and praying through each room, peace returned.

Key Memory Verses

- 1 John 4:1

- John 16:13

- 1 Corinthians 2:14

- Romans 8:6

Reflection Questions

- Are you growing in discernment or reacting in suspicion?

- How can you guard your home and heart against spiritual deception better?

- How can discernment be cultivated, and what role does intimacy with God play in its growth?

Why is it important to test spiritual experiences, and how can wisdom help discern whether they are from God?

In what ways can you guard your spiritual atmosphere with vigilance and intentionality?

Exercises

1. **Discernment Journal**: Reflect on a past decision—was it discernment or suspicion? What was the fruit?

2. **Spirit Test Practice**: Take a current spiritual teaching or influence and test it against Scripture.

3. **Atmosphere Audit**: List everything that influences your heart daily (music, media, people). Ask God what needs to stay or go.

Discussion Questions

- How can you tell the difference between human suspicion and spiritual discernment?

- What role does Scripture play in your discernment process?

- How do you cultivate a spiritually healthy atmosphere in your home and heart?

Prayer Guide

- **Prayer for Discernment and Spiritual Guidance**: "Holy Spirit, I ask You to sharpen my discernment. Teach me to recognize what is from You and what is not. Help me to walk in truth, to test everything by Your Word, and to guard the spiritual gates of my heart. Keep me sensitive to Your voice and rooted in wisdom. In Jesus's name, Amen."

Topics Covered

- Difference between suspicion and discernment

- The role of the Holy Spirit

- Testing the spirits (1 John 4:1)

- Protecting your spiritual atmosphere

Chapter 14:
Guarding Your
Home and Family

Key Scriptures

- *Joshua 24:15—"As for me and my house, we will serve the Lord."*

- *Proverbs 24:3–4—"By wisdom a house is built, and through understanding it is established; through knowledge its rooms are filled with rare and beautiful treasures."*

Overview

The home is meant to be a sanctuary of peace, safety, and spiritual growth. As spiritual leaders and stewards, we must intentionally protect our homes and families from spiritual compromise. This chapter focuses on creating a Christ-centered atmosphere, identifying open doors to the enemy, and establishing prayer and worship as pillars in the home.

Expanded Study

1. Spiritual Responsibility in the Home

Every believer has a role in shaping the spiritual tone of the household. Whether you are a parent, spouse, sibling, or single adult, your commitment to honoring God in your space makes a difference.

Practical Insight

- Make time for family prayer and devotions.

- Set boundaries about what is watched, listened to, and invited into your home.

Example: A couple who noticed their children having nightmares began praying nightly as a family, playing worship music, and removing dark content from the house. Peace returned.

2. Identifying and Closing Spiritual Gateways

The enemy often looks for legal entry points into households—bitterness, occult objects, unrepentant sin, or relational strife.

Checklist of Common Open Doors

- Unforgiveness or ongoing conflict

- Involvement in the occult (e.g., horoscopes, witchcraft, crystals)

- Sexual immorality or substance abuse

- Music, movies, or games with demonic themes

Steps to Close the Doors

- Repent for any involvement or agreement with darkness.

- Remove any items tied to spiritual compromise.

- Pray over and anoint each room in your home (James 5:14).

3. Establishing a Culture of Worship and Prayer

Prayer and worship invite God's presence and build spiritual protection.

Practical Ways to Implement

- Play worship music daily.

- Designate a prayer space or family altar.

- Declare Scriptures over your household (Psalm 91, Ephesians 6).

Example: A widow who lived alone kept a prayer journal and regularly

anointed her home. She noticed a spirit of peace and clarity remain despite
external trials.

---

4. Teaching and Modeling Faith to Children

Children absorb more from what we model than what we say. Raising
spiritually aware children means teaching them to pray, discern, and value
God's Word.

Deuteronomy 6:6–7—*"These commandments...impress them on your
children...talk about them when you sit at home and when you walk along
the road."*

Practical Insight

- Pray with and for your children daily.

- Encourage open conversation about God and spiritual questions.

- Involve children in acts of worship, service, and Scripture reading.

Key Memory Verses

- Joshua 24:15

- Proverbs 24:3–4

- Psalm 91:1–2

- Deuteronomy 6:6–7

Reflection Questions

- What kind of spiritual atmosphere exists in your home?

- Are there areas where compromise has crept in?

- What steps can you take today to guard and consecrate your household to the Lord?

- How can filling your home with God's presence make it a place of peace, protection, and growth?

....

....

....

....

....

- In what ways do the things that enter your home—through entertainment, language, or behavior—impact you spiritually?

....

....

....

....

- Why is your home considered your first ministry, and how can you build it on the Rock?

....

....

....

....

Exercises

1. **Spiritual House Audit**: Examine your home for anything spiritually compromising (books, shows, music, objects). Remove anything that doesn't honor God.

2. **Family Altar**: Establish a time for daily or weekly family worship and prayer.

3. **Legacy Letter**: Write a letter of faith and blessing to your children or family members, declaring God's promises over their lives.

Discussion Questions

- What influences are shaping your home spiritually?

- How do you model Christ to your family?

- What's one area where your household can grow spiritually this week?

Prayer Guide

Prayer of Household Dedication and Spiritual Leadership: "Lord, I dedicate my home to You. Cleanse it of anything that opposes Your Spirit. Help me lead with love, humility, and faith. Let our home be a place of Your presence and power. Teach me to guard the spiritual atmosphere and disciple my family well. In Jesus's name, Amen."

Topics Covered

- Spiritual responsibility in the home

- Identifying and closing spiritual gateways

- Establishing a culture of worship and prayer

- Teaching and modeling faith to children

Chapter 15:
Watchfulness and Warfare in Daily Life

Key Scriptures

- *1 Peter 5:8—"Be sober-minded; be watchful. Your adversary the devil prowls around like a roaring lion, seeking someone to devour."*

- *Ephesians 6:18—"Praying at all times in the Spirit, with all prayer and supplication. To that end, keep alert..."*

Overview

Spiritual warfare is not just an occasional battle; it's a lifestyle of vigilance, prayer, and intentional living. This chapter equips believers to remain spiritually alert in everyday life, identifying subtle attacks and remaining anchored in Christ through routine disciplines and readiness.

Expanded Study

1. Living a Watchful Life

Watchfulness is a spiritual posture. It means being alert to the enemy's schemes while anchored in God's peace.

Practical Insight

- Begin each day with prayer and spiritual alignment.

- Pay attention to spiritual atmosphere shifts—sudden fear, strife, or temptation may be indicators.

Example: A woman would feel overwhelming discouragement every time she prepared to evangelize. By recognizing it as a pattern of spiritual opposition, she countered it with praise and boldness.

2. Recognizing Subtle Spiritual Attacks

Not all attacks are dramatic—many are disguised as distraction, offense, or emotional fatigue.

Common Subtle Attacks

- Emotional weariness that distances you from prayer

- Busy schedules that crowd out spiritual focus

- Irritability or offense that damages relationships

Counterstrategy

- Guard your time with God like a treasure.

- Don't ignore little spiritual red flags—address them early with prayer.

3. Daily Disciplines for Spiritual Strength

Winning battles starts with strong daily rhythms.

Daily Practices

- **Prayer and Bible Reading:** Align your mind and spirit with truth.

- **Worship:** Lifts your spirit and invites God's presence.

- **Gratitude Journaling:** Keeps your heart anchored in faith.

Example: A father wrote down three things he was grateful for daily. It helped him stay hopeful even when facing financial pressures.

4. Keeping the Armor of God On

Ephesians 6 reminds us to "put on" the full armor—not occasionally, but daily.

Practical Insight

- Verbally pray through each piece of the armor in the morning (Ephesians 6:10–18).

- Teach your children or spouse to do the same. It fosters unity and defense.

Example Prayer: "Lord, I put on the belt of truth, breastplate of righteousness, shoes of peace, shield of faith, helmet of salvation, and I take up the sword of the Spirit. I stand firm today in You."

Key Memory Verses

- 1 Peter 5:8

- Ephesians 6:18

- Colossians 4:2

- James 4:7

- Are you alert to the enemy's tactics in your daily life? Alertness in the Spirit protects us from traps we didn't see coming.

- How can you cultivate spiritual discipline and attentiveness in practical ways?

- How does consistency in spiritual disciplines help build resistance against the enemy's schemes?

What does it mean to "live with your armor on" by choosing Christ daily in your thoughts, words, and deeds?

....

....

....

....

....

Exercises

1. **Discernment Journal**: Reflect each evening for a week—were there any subtle attacks (e.g., discouragement, distraction, confusion)? How did you respond?

2. **Armor Checklist**: Create a visual chart of the armor of God and commit to meditating on one piece each day for a week.

3. **Spiritual Strength Plan**: Set daily goals for Bible reading, prayer time, and gratitude journaling. Track your consistency.

Discussion Questions

- What does living "watchfully" look like in daily life?

- How can we detect subtle attacks before they take root?

- Which spiritual discipline do you struggle with most—and why?

Prayer Guide

Prayer of Spiritual Alertness and Warfare: "Lord, help me to stay spiritually alert and aware of the enemy's schemes. Strengthen me through Your Word, prayer, and faithful obedience. Let me never grow numb or complacent in my walk with You. Equip me daily with Your armor, and help me live a life that honors and glorifies You. In Jesus's name, Amen."

Topics Covered

- Living a watchful life

- Recognizing subtle spiritual attacks

- Daily disciplines for spiritual strength

- Keeping the armor of God on

Chapter 16:
Staying Battle-Ready in Every Season

Key Scriptures

- *2 Timothy 4:2 – "Be ready in season and out of season."*

- *Ecclesiastes 3:1 – "There is a time for everything, and a season for every activity under the heavens."*

Overview

Spiritual warfare doesn't pause with life's seasons. Whether you're in a time of harvest or hardship, the enemy looks for opportunity. This chapter will help you recognize seasonal shifts in the spirit, maintain your strength, and apply practical strategies to stay spiritually prepared in any circumstance.

Expanded Study

1. Recognizing Spiritual Seasons

Life has rhythms—so does the spiritual realm. Discernment helps us know whether we're in a time of planting, pruning, rest, or warfare.

Examples of Spiritual Seasons

- **Wilderness (testing):** like Jesus in Matthew 4

- **Harvest (fruitfulness):** like Acts 2 after Pentecost

- **Transition:** like Abraham moving to a new land (Genesis 12)

Practical Insight

- Ask the Lord to reveal the current spiritual season you're in.

- Adjust expectations and prayer focus accordingly.

2. Maintaining Vigilance in Quiet Seasons

Sometimes when life is peaceful, we let our guard down. These are the times to build reserves of faith.

Example: A mother found that when her schedule slowed, she spent less time in prayer. She later realized this spiritual laxity made her more vulnerable during sudden trials.

Practical Tips

- Stay consistent in prayer even when things are going well.

- Don't confuse ease with the absence of spiritual warfare.

3. Drawing Strength in Seasons of Intense Battle

In hard times, you may feel spiritually drained. Yet these are the moments to lean in harder to God's presence.

Practical Insight

- Fast and pray as led (Mark 9:29).

- Surround yourself with godly voices and prophetic encouragement.

- Declare God's promises aloud daily.

Example: During a season of unemployment, a man kept Psalm 23 on his wall and read it aloud every morning. It carried him with peace through financial uncertainty.

4. Preparing Ahead for Spiritual Shifts

The wise believer doesn't wait for a crisis to prepare; they stay equipped.

Practical Insight

- Keep a prayer journal tracking God's answers and victories.

- Memorize key warfare Scriptures (Ephesians 6, Psalm 91, Romans 8).

- Regularly review your spiritual goals and disciplines.

Key Memory Verses

- 2 Timothy 4:2

- Ecclesiastes 3:1

- Mark 9:29

- Psalm 23:4

Reflection Questions

- What season are you currently in spiritually?

....

....

....

- How can you stay alert and equipped whether in abundance or adversity?

....

....

....

- How can understanding that not all battles are punishments, but often preparations, change the way you approach challenges?

- In what ways does God use every season of life for our transformation?

- Why are quiet seasons just as important as stormy ones, and how do they help build deep roots in your faith?

Exercises

1. **Season Assessment**: Reflect—What spiritual season are you currently in? Write down signs that point to this.

2. **Preparation Plan**: What spiritual disciplines can you strengthen now to prepare for the next season?

3. **Testimony Timeline**: Draw a timeline of your life's spiritual seasons. Mark the fruit and lessons of each.

Discussion Questions

- How do you know what spiritual season you're in?

- What are the dangers of misjudging or resisting your season?

- How can we support each other during different spiritual seasons?

Prayer Guide

"Father, thank You for the spiritual seasons You've ordained in my life. Help me discern my current season and respond with faith and obedience. In quiet seasons, help me grow deeper. In battles, help me stand firm. Prepare me for the transitions ahead and teach me to walk with You in every moment. In Jesus's name, Amen."

Topics Covered

- Recognizing spiritual seasons

- Maintaining vigilance in quiet seasons

- Drawing strength in seasons of intense battle

- Preparing ahead for spiritual shifts

Chapter 17:
Spiritual Warfare and Mental Health

Key Scriptures

- *2 Corinthians 10:5—"We take captive every thought to make it obedient to Christ."*

- *Isaiah 26:3—"You will keep in perfect peace those whose minds are steadfast, because they trust in you."*

Overview

Mental and emotional well-being is not separate from spiritual warfare. Many believers struggle silently with anxiety, depression, fear, and intrusive thoughts—all of which can be spiritual battlegrounds. The enemy works through deception, fear, and lies to control thoughts and behaviors. Victory begins with renewing the mind, replacing lies with truth, and aligning with God's Word. This chapter explores how to partner with God's truth to maintain mental strength, peace, and clarity in the midst of spiritual conflict.

Expanded Study

1. Understanding the Mind as a Battlefield

The mind is often where spiritual warfare begins. Satan's strategy is to implant lies and distort perceptions to keep believers bound in fear, shame, or hopelessness.

Practical Insight

- Recognize that not every thought is your own—some are suggestions from the enemy.

- Ask: "Is this thought lifegiving and aligned with God's Word?"

Example: A man plagued with constant thoughts of failure realized they contradicted Philippians 1:6. He began to speak that verse over his life daily and found peace increasing.

2. Replacing Lies with Truth

Spiritual transformation happens when truth takes the place of lies.

Process of Renewal

- Identify the lie ("I'll never change.")

- Reject it in prayer ("In Jesus's name, I renounce this lie.")

- Replace it with truth ("I am a new creation in Christ" [2 Corinthians 5:17].)

Tools

- Truth declaration cards

- Biblical affirmations

- Journaling thoughts and Scripture responses

3. Breaking Agreement with Fear and Anxiety

Fear is one of Satan's strongest tools to paralyze believers. Anxiety can be rooted in both physiological and spiritual causes, but God offers peace that surpasses understanding.

Philippians 4:6–7—*"Do not be anxious about anything... and the peace of God... will guard your hearts and your minds in Christ Jesus."*

Practical Tips

- Daily declarations of peace (Isaiah 41:10, Psalm 23:4)

- Breath prayers: "Jesus, I trust You."

- Worship and gratitude as tools to shift atmosphere

4. Combining Spiritual and Practical Support

God uses multiple tools to bring wholeness—including counseling, medication, support groups, and community.

Example: A young woman battling panic attacks found freedom through inner healing prayer, therapy, and practical sleep/diet changes. Wholeness came through a combination of spiritual and natural strategies.

Encouragement

- Don't be ashamed to seek help.

- Healing is a journey, and God walks with you through every step.

Key Memory Verses

- 2 Corinthians 10:5

- Isaiah 26:3

- Philippians 4:6–7

- 2 Timothy 1:7

Reflection Questions

- What recurring thoughts or mental battles do you face?

....

....

....

....

How can you align your thinking with God's truth and receive His peace today?

....

....

....

....

How do your beliefs influence the way you live your daily life?

....

....

....

....

Why is it important not to accept every thought, and how can you test them by God's Word?

....

....

....

....

In what ways does healing in the mind involve both spiritual and practical steps, and how does God use various tools in this process?

....

....

....

....

....

Exercises

1. **Thought Capture**: List recurring negative or anxious thoughts. Find a verse that speaks truth over each one.

2. **Confession Routine**: Write three truth statements based on Scripture and say them daily.

3. **Support System Map**: Identify trusted individuals, mentors, or professionals you can turn to for mental/emotional support.

Discussion Questions

What lies have you believed that shaped your decisions or self-image?

How can we recognize when fear is trying to control us?

In what ways can the church support those struggling with mental battles?

Prayer Guide

"Lord, I surrender my thoughts to You. Help me recognize and reject the lies of the enemy. Replace them with Your truth. Give me the courage to break agreement with fear and anxiety. Fill my mind with peace and clarity, and guide me to the right support and strategies to walk in mental freedom. In Jesus's name, Amen."

Topics Covered

- Understanding the mind as a battlefield

- Replacing lies with truth

- Breaking agreement with fear and anxiety

- Combining spiritual and practical support

Chapter 18:
Spiritual Warfare in Ministry and Leadership

Key Scriptures

- *James 3:1—"Not many of you should become teachers, my fellow believers, because you know that we who teach will be judged more strictly."*

- *Acts 20:28—"Keep watch over yourselves and all the flock of which the Holy Spirit has made you overseers."*

- *Hebrews 13:17—"Have confidence in your leaders and submit to their authority, because they keep watch over you as those who must give an account."*

Overview

Leaders and those involved in ministry carry unique responsibilities—and face targeted spiritual warfare. Whether in the home, church, or community, spiritual influence carries weight and responsibility. Leaders must remain vigilant, protect their anointing, and lean on God while serving others. This chapter addresses the weight of spiritual leadership, how to guard your calling, avoid common pitfalls, and walk in integrity while under pressure.

Expanded Study

1. The Weight of Spiritual Influence

With great responsibility comes spiritual scrutiny. Leaders set the spiritual climate for those they serve.

Practical Insight

- Prioritize your personal walk with God over public ministry.

- Regularly evaluate your heart for pride, burnout, or hidden compromise.

Example: A pastor confessed to leading out of performance instead of

presence. By restoring his daily prayer life, his joy and effectiveness returned.

---

2. Common Attacks Against Leaders

Satan aims to discredit those in visible roles. Understanding the patterns of
attack can help leaders stay alert.

Tactics Include

- Isolation and burnout

- Moral temptation and discouragement

- Division in leadership teams

Strategy

- Build a trusted inner circle for accountability.

- Take regular sabbath rests and retreats.

- Have spiritual mentors or overseers.

---

3. Protecting the Anointing

Your calling must be guarded with humility and discipline.

Biblical Model

- David remained humble even after being anointed king (1 Samuel
  16).

- Jesus often withdrew to pray alone (Luke 5:16).

Practical Disciplines

- Maintain spiritual hunger—never lead on empty.

- Stay teachable and correctable.

- Do not neglect your family for ministry.

---

4. Spiritual Warfare in Serving Others

Ministering deliverance, healing, or preaching truth often stirs opposition.

Preparation for Ministry Warfare

- Fast and pray before key ministry moments.

- Armor up spiritually before preaching or serving.

- Discern spiritual atmosphere and respond with authority.

Example: A worship leader noticed extreme heaviness before certain services. After gathering a prayer team to intercede beforehand, a breakthrough began to flow.

Key Memory Verses

- James 3:1

- Acts 20:28

- Luke 5:16

- 1 Samuel 16:7

- Are you leading from a place of overflow or depletion?

....

....

....

....

- How can you guard your calling and prioritize God's presence over performance?

....

....

....

....

- How does anointing attract spiritual warfare, and why is it important to stay close to the Anointed One?

....

....

....

....

- Why are leaders not immune to attack, and how can support, rest, and covering help them?

- In what ways does your leadership influence flow most effectively from intimacy with God?

Exercises

1. **Leadership Journal**: Reflect on your leadership responsibilities. What areas are most spiritually draining? How are you replenishing them?

2. **Intercession List**: Create a prayer list for those under your leadership and commit to praying regularly.

3. **Accountability Check**: Identify who you can go to for counsel and accountability. Reach out this week.

Discussion Questions

- What spiritual attacks do leaders commonly face?

- How can a leader guard their heart and anointing?

- What does healthy, Christ-like leadership look like to you?

Prayer Guide

Prayer for Leadership, Strength, and Spiritual Covering: "Father, thank You for the privilege of influence. Help me lead with humility, integrity, and wisdom. Protect me from pride, burnout, and compromise. Strengthen me in battle and fill me with fresh oil daily. May I lead others in Your strength and point them always to You. In Jesus's name, Amen."

Topics Covered

- The weight of spiritual influence

- Common attacks against leaders

- Protecting the anointing

- Spiritual warfare in serving others

Chapter 19:
Spiritual Gifts and Warfare

Key Scriptures

- *1 Corinthians 12:7—"Now to each one the manifestation of the Spirit is given for the common good."*

- *Romans 12:6—"We have different gifts, according to the grace given to each of us."*

Overview

Spiritual gifts are not just for edification but also for equipping the Church in spiritual warfare. They are divine tools for building the Body of Christ and advancing God's Kingdom. In spiritual warfare, they are strategic weapons that bring breakthrough, healing, discernment, and direction. This chapter explores how discernment, prophecy, intercession, and other spiritual gifts can be strategically employed in spiritual battle, and how to cultivate, steward, and protect them.

Expanded Study

1. The Purpose of Spiritual Gifts in Warfare

Spiritual gifts are divine tools to edify, protect, and advance the Church. When used rightly, they expose darkness, build unity, and strengthen believers against demonic schemes.

Examples

- A word of knowledge can reveal hidden strongholds.

- The gift of discernment can protect from deceptive spirits.

- Prophecy can release breakthrough and direction in seasons of confusion.

Practical Insight

- View your gift as a weapon to build others up, not just personal identity.

- Ask God daily to show how He wants to use your gift in prayer and ministry.

---

2. Discerning and Activating Your Gifts

Many believers don't recognize their gifts or struggle to walk in them. Activating them starts with awareness, faith, and practice.

Ways to Discover and Use Your Gift

- Study Romans 12, 1 Corinthians 12, and Ephesians 4.

- Ask mature believers or mentors what they see in you.

- Step out in faith during small group settings or prayer times.

Example: A quiet woman who felt insignificant discovered she had a strong gift of intercession when her prayers began breaking spiritual heaviness over others. She became a powerful prayer leader.

---

3. Guarding Against Pride, Fear, and Comparison

Spiritual gifts must be stewarded with humility and love. Pride can misuse gifts; fear can suppress them; comparison can kill joy.

1 Corinthians 13 reminds us that gifts without love are nothing.

Practical Guardrails

- Stay accountable to leadership and community.

- Celebrate others' gifts without comparison.

- Remain teachable and open to correction.

4. Using Your Gift Strategically in Battle

Each gift has warfare applications:

- **Prophecy:** Releases truth and direction; dismantles lies.

- **Healing:** Demonstrates the Kingdom and breaks infirmity.

- **Intercession:** Builds walls of protection and disarms attacks.

- **Discernment:** Detects spiritual shifts and enemy plans.

- **Teaching:** Equips believers with solid doctrine to resist deception.

Example: A man with a teaching gift began hosting weekly Bible study in his home. Over time, attendees saw freedom from confusion and false teachings.

Key Memory Verses

- 1 Corinthians 12:7

- Romans 12:6

- Ephesians 4:11–13

- 1 Peter 4:10

Reflection Questions

- What gifts has God given you?

....

....

....

- Are you actively using them in a way that equips others for spiritual battle?

....

....

....

....

- What steps can you take to develop and deploy your gifts more effectively?

....

....

....

....

- How do your spiritual gifts point to God's glory rather than define your identity?

In what ways does spiritual warfare reveal the timing and necessity of your gifts?

Why is it important to use the gifts God gives you in faith, knowing He has a purpose for them?

Exercises

1. **Gift Discovery Quiz**: Take a spiritual gifts assessment and reflect on the results. Journal how each gift might be used in warfare.

2. **Bold Gift Activation**: Identify a need (in church, family, or community) and use one of your gifts intentionally this week.

3. **Comparison Detox**: Write a list of spiritual lies you've believed (e.g., "I'm not gifted," "Their gift is better"). Replace each with Scripture-based truth.

Discussion Questions

- How have you seen spiritual gifts used effectively in warfare?

- What holds you back from fully using your gifts?

- How can the church help believers activate and mature their gifts?

Prayer Guide

"Holy Spirit, thank You for the gifts You've placed in me. Help me to discern, embrace, and activate them for Your glory. Remove fear, pride, and comparison from my heart. Let me serve boldly and faithfully, using what You've given to destroy the works of darkness and lift up Your name. In Jesus's name, Amen."

Topics Covered

- The purpose of spiritual gifts in warfare

- Discerning and activating your gifts

- Guarding against pride, fear, and comparison

- Using your gift strategically in battle

Chapter 20:
Intercession and Strategic Prayer

Key Scriptures

- *Ezekiel 22:30—"I looked for someone among them who would build up the wall and stand before me in the gap..."*

- *James 5:16—"The prayer of a righteous person is powerful and effective."*

Overview

Intercession is one of the most powerful tools in spiritual warfare. God calls believers to stand in the gap on behalf of others, regions, and situations. This chapter focuses on the strategic role of intercession, how to develop a lifestyle of prayer, and practical frameworks for praying effectively against demonic activity.

Expanded Study

1. The Call to Stand in the Gap

To intercede means to plead on behalf of someone else. In Scripture, God often sought intercessors to withhold judgment or release His will.

Example: Abraham interceded for Sodom (Genesis 18). Moses interceded for Israel (Exodus 32).

Practical Insight

- Ask God regularly: "Who or what do You want me to stand in the gap for today?"

- Be willing to labor in prayer until breakthrough comes.

2. Types of Intercessory Prayer

Not all intercession looks the same. God may lead you into different types:

- **Warfare Intercession:** Breaking strongholds over people, places, or churches.

- **Prophetic Intercession:** Praying what you sense from the Holy Spirit.

- **Priestly Intercession:** Bringing the needs of others before God like a priest.

Example: A woman was woken up nightly to pray for a friend in another country. Months later, she learned that friend was facing intense persecution during those exact times.

3. Prayer Strategies in Warfare

Strategic intercession requires intentionality, preparation, and discernment.

Prayer Tools

- **Prayer Maps: Assign specific topics, needs, or people to focus on each day.**

- **Prayer Declarations:** Speaking God's Word over situations.

- **Targeted Lists:** Names, cities, ministries, or issues to cover regularly.

Example: A small group adopted their local school in prayer. Over time, bullying decreased and two teachers gave their lives to Christ.

4. Praying from a Place of Victory

Effective intercession doesn't beg; it agrees with what Christ has already done.

Ephesians 2:6—You are seated with Christ.

Practical Tips

- Begin with praise and thanksgiving.

- Declare the promises of God, not just the problems.

- Listen for Holy Spirit direction more than speaking long prayers.

Key Memory Verses

- Ezekiel 22:30

- James 5:16

- Ephesians 2:6

- Isaiah 62:6–7

Reflection Questions

- Do you see yourself as an intercessor?

- Who or what is God calling you to cover in prayer today?

....

....

....

....

- How can you build intentional prayer strategies that result in breakthroughs?

....

....

....

....

- How does agreement in prayer multiply spiritual power, as described in Deuteronomy 32:30?

....

....

....

....

- What are the key elements of true agreement, and why are humility, unity, and shared commitment to God's truth important?

- Why are prayer partnerships not just helpful but essential for spiritual growth and effectiveness?

Exercises

1. **Prayer Partner Challenge**: Find someone to pray with for seven consecutive days. Keep a journal of what you pray and any insights received.

2. **Unity Check**: Ask the Lord to reveal any relationships where your agreement is broken. Pray for healing and restoration.

3. **Word-Based Agreement**: Choose a promise from Scripture and come into agreement with a friend or group to pray that Word into your lives.

Discussion Questions

- Why is intercession critical to spiritual warfare?

- Who has interceded for you in the past?

- How have you experienced the power of agreement in prayer?

- What blocks unity in prayer partnerships or churches?

- Why is agreement with heaven's will necessary for effective warfare?

Prayer Guide

"Lord, teach me the power of agreement in Your presence. Forgive me where I've walked in pride or disunity. Help me find godly prayer partners and walk in unity with others and with Your Word. Release heaven's authority as we align our hearts and prayers together. In Jesus's name, Amen."

Topics Covered

- The call to stand in the gap

- Types of intercessory prayer

- Prayer strategies in warfare

- Praying from a place of victory

Chapter 21:
The Church in Action—Advancing God's Kingdom Together

Key Scriptures

- *Matthew 5:14–16—"You are the light of the world. A city set on a hill cannot be hidden... let your light shine before others, that they may see your good deeds and glorify your Father in heaven."*

- *Acts 2:42–47—"They devoted themselves to the apostles' teaching and to fellowship, to the breaking of bread and to prayer... and the Lord added to their number daily those who were being saved."*

- *Romans 12:4–5—"For just as each of us has one body with many members... so in Christ we, though many, form one body, and each member belongs to all the others."*

Overview

The Church is not a passive audience—it is an *active force for transformation*. As the Body of Christ, we are called to advance God's Kingdom by being His hands, feet, and voice in the world. Every act of love, service, and prayer contributes to spiritual victory over darkness.

This chapter explores how believers can function as a united, Spirit-filled community that carries God's presence into families, cities, and nations. The Church in action doesn't just defend truth—it *demonstrates* it with compassion and power.

Expanded Study

1. The Church as God's Living Body

The Church represents Christ on earth—His compassion, justice, and authority working through people. When believers operate in unity, they become the visible expression of God's Kingdom.

Example: In Acts 2, the early Church shared resources, prayed together, and displayed radical love. This unity drew many to salvation and expanded the Kingdom rapidly.

Practical Insight:

- View your local church as Christ's hands extended to the community.

- Serve with the mindset that *your ministry meets spiritual and physical needs alike.*

---

2. The Power of Kingdom Influence

The Church is called not only to gather but also to influence society—through integrity, service, and Spirit-led boldness. Wherever the Church is active, darkness loses ground.

Example: The believers in Antioch (Acts 11:26) became a model of Kingdom influence—sharing the Gospel across cultures and showing mercy to the poor.

Practical Insight:

- Let your church's presence bring light to schools, workplaces, and government.

- Promote justice, mercy, and compassion as forms of spiritual warfare.

---

3. Equipping and Sending Disciples

God never designed the Church to be a place of comfort, but a *launching ground* for disciples. True spiritual maturity leads to mission.

Scripture Insight: Jesus trained His disciples and sent them out two by two (Luke 10:1–3). Likewise, churches should raise up believers to evangelize, mentor, and serve.

Practical Tools for Churches:

- Develop leadership and discipleship tracks.

- Encourage every member to discover and use their spiritual gifts.

- Celebrate testimonies of transformation and service.

Example: A small church trained members in evangelism, resulting in dozens of new believers and community outreach programs.

---

4. Advancing God's Kingdom in the World

The Church's mission extends beyond the walls. It's global, cultural, and eternal. Prayer, service, and justice initiatives reveal God's rule over every sphere of life.

Examples:

- Churches partnering in mission trips or feeding programs.

- Believers mentoring youth or standing for truth in media and politics.

- Worship events uniting multiple congregations to declare Christ's reign.

Practical Insight:

- Ask: "How can our church bless our city this month?"

- Partner with other ministries to multiply impact.

- Live on mission daily—your workplace, classroom, or home can be your mission field.

- Matthew 5:14–16

- Acts 2:42–47

- Romans 12:4–5

- Luke 10:1–3

Reflection Questions

- How can you personally help your church impact your community?

- What does it mean to you that *you are the light of the world*?

- How can your local church become a sending center rather than just a gathering space?

- What part of God's mission stirs your heart the most?

- How can your gifts help advance the Kingdom where you live?

Exercises

- **Mission Map:** Identify one need in your community and brainstorm how your church could meet it.

- **Service Challenge:** Volunteer for an outreach, youth ministry, or prayer initiative.

- **Kingdom Partner:** Connect with another believer or church to collaborate on a good work.

- **Scripture Walk:** Walk through your neighborhood declaring God's promises over homes, schools, and families.

Discussion Questions

- How can the Church balance preaching truth with showing love in action?

- What would it look like if every believer lived "on mission" daily?

- How can unity between churches change the atmosphere of a city?

- What role does your generation play in advancing God's Kingdom?

Prayer Guide

Prayer for Mission, Compassion, and Unity: "Lord Jesus, thank You for calling Your Church to action. Fill us with Your Spirit and compassion to reach the lost and serve the broken. Unite us in purpose and power so that Your Kingdom advances through every act of love, prayer, and service. Use us as vessels of Your glory—here and around the world. Amen."

Prayer for Boldness and Influence: "Father, make us a Church that shines Your light boldly and consistently. Let our works bring others to glorify You."

Topics Covered

- The Church as God's living Body

- The power of Kingdom influence

- Equipping and sending disciples

- Advancing God's Kingdom in the world

Chapter 22:
Living in Victory: Maintaining Spiritual Freedom

Key Scriptures

- *Romans 8:37—"No, in all these things we are more than conquerors through him who loved us."*

- *1 John 5:4—"For everyone born of God overcomes the world. This is the victory that has overcome the world, even our faith."*

- *2 Corinthians 2:14—"But thanks be to God, who always leads us as captives in Christ's triumphal procession and uses us to spread the aroma of the knowledge of him everywhere."*

Overview

Victory is not just a destination; it's a daily lifestyle rooted in our identity in Christ. Victory in spiritual warfare is not merely about winning battles; it's about living every day in the freedom and authority that Christ has provided. Understanding your spiritual position equips you to overcome setbacks and spiritual attacks while living in freedom and authority. This chapter focuses on how believers can maintain their spiritual freedom, cultivate a victorious mindset, and walk confidently in their identity as conquerors through Christ.

Expanded Study

1. Understanding Your Position in Christ

Victory begins with a clear understanding of who you are in Jesus. You are no longer a victim but a victor, seated with Christ in heavenly places (Ephesians 2:6).

Practical Insight

- Regularly remind yourself of your new identity as a child of God.

- Reject lies that say you are weak or defeated.

- Meditate on verses that affirm your victory and authority.

Example: A believer struggling with guilt found freedom by daily declaring Romans 8:1: *"There is no condemnation for those who are in Christ Jesus."*

2. Cultivating a Lifestyle of Victory

Victory is maintained through intentional habits and spiritual disciplines that reinforce your freedom.

Key Practices

- **Daily Prayer and Worship:** Keeping close fellowship with God.

- **Scripture Meditation:** Letting God's Word renew your mind.

- **Faith-Filled Confession:** Speaking truth over circumstances.

- **Regular Fellowship:** Surrounding yourself with encouragers.

Example: A woman who was often discouraged started a daily routine of Scripture memorization and prayer. Over time, her faith grew stronger, and she experienced lasting peace.

3. Overcoming Setbacks and Attacks

Even victorious believers face challenges. Understanding how to respond to setbacks is vital.

Responses to Spiritual Setbacks

- **Repent and Restore:** Quickly confess and return to God's grace.

- **Seek Support:** Reach out to trusted believers or mentors.

- **Reaffirm God's Promises:** Declare victory in Christ aloud.

- ☉ **Remain Persistent:** Don't give up; spiritual warfare is ongoing.

Example: After a period of spiritual dryness, a man renewed his commitment to prayer and fellowship. He regained joy and strength to continue standing firm.

---

4. Walking in Freedom and Authority Daily

Your victory in Christ gives you authority over the enemy. Walking in this authority requires confidence and obedience.

Practical Tips

- ☉ Use the name of Jesus boldly when facing temptation or attack.

- ☉ Apply the finished work of the cross—know that Jesus has disarmed the enemy.

- ☉ Guard your heart and mind with the armor of God.

Example: When confronted with fear, a believer would say, "In Jesus's name, fear must leave." Over time, this practice broke the power of fear in her life.

Key Memory Verses

- ☉ Romans 8:37

- ☉ 1 John 5:4

- ☉ Ephesians 2:6

- ☉ 2 Corinthians 5:17

Reflection Questions

- Are you living daily as a conqueror in Christ?

....

....

....

....

- What spiritual disciplines can you cultivate to maintain your victory?

....

....

....

....

- How will you respond the next time you face a spiritual or personal attack?

....

....

....

....

- In what ways does your authority in Christ depend on your position in Him rather than your performance?

____

____

____

____

- Why is living in victory dependent on having a renewed mind and a submitted heart?

____

____

____

____

- How can setbacks become opportunities for a comeback when you stay connected to God?

____

____

____

____

Exercises

1. **Identity Declarations**: Write five biblical truths about who you are in Christ. Speak them aloud every morning this week.

2. **Victory Inventory**: Reflect on a recent spiritual setback. What did you learn? What truth can you now walk in more confidently?

3. **Freedom Habits**: List three spiritual disciplines you need to strengthen. Make a seven-day plan to practice each one.

4. **Remember God's Faithfulness:** List God's faithfulness in past seasons.

Discussion Questions

- What does it mean to live *from* victory instead of fighting *for* it?

- How does your position in Christ affect your daily decisions?

- What disciplines help you maintain spiritual authority and freedom?

- What helps you stay strong when breakthrough is delayed?

Prayer Guide

Prayer of Victory and Spiritual Authority: "Lord Jesus, thank You for the victory You won for me at the cross. Help me live each day aware of my position in You. Strengthen me to walk in truth, guard my heart against lies, and lead me in freedom and purpose. May I reflect Your authority and love wherever I go. In Your name, Amen."

Prayer for Endurance and Perseverance: "Lord, strengthen me to endure and not give up."

Topics Covered

- Understanding your position in Christ

- Cultivating a lifestyle of victory

- Overcoming setbacks and attacks

- Walking in freedom and authority daily

Chapter 23:
The Role of the Holy Spirit in Spiritual Warfare

Key Scriptures

- *John 14:26—"But the Advocate, the Holy Spirit, whom the Father will send in my name, will teach you all things and will remind you of everything I have said to you."*

- *Romans 8:26—"In the same way, the Spirit helps us in our weakness. We do not know what we ought to pray for, but the Spirit himself intercedes for us through wordless groans."*

Overview

The Holy Spirit is the believer's essential companion in spiritual warfare—empowering, guiding, and interceding on our behalf. This chapter explores how the Spirit works in our lives during battle, equipping us with wisdom, strength, and victory.

Expanded Study

1. Empowerment for Battle

The Holy Spirit provides the power and boldness needed to stand against spiritual attacks. Without His presence, spiritual warfare can feel overwhelming.

Example: At Pentecost (Acts 2), believers received the Holy Spirit and were empowered to preach boldly and perform miracles despite opposition.

Practical Insight

- Pray daily for the filling and empowerment of the Holy Spirit (Ephesians 5:18).

- Depend on His strength rather than your own.

2. Guidance and Wisdom

The Spirit guides believers into truth and strategy for spiritual battles. He reveals the enemy's tactics and how to respond.

John 16:13 promises the Spirit will guide into all truth.

Example: Jesus, led by the Spirit, knew when to confront and when to withdraw during His temptation in the wilderness.

Practical Insight

- Cultivate sensitivity to the Spirit's promptings through prayer and stillness.

- Seek His guidance before engaging in spiritual warfare or ministry.

3. Intercession on Our Behalf

When we don't know how or what to pray, the Spirit intercedes with groanings beyond words (Romans 8:26). This supernatural help sustains us in prolonged spiritual battles.

Practical Insight

- Trust the Spirit's intercession when your prayers feel weak or dry.

- Join in with the Spirit's groans through persistent prayer.

4. Filling with the Fruit of the Spirit

The fruit of the Spirit—love, joy, peace, patience, kindness, goodness, faithfulness, gentleness, and self-control—are essential weapons in warfare that disarm the enemy's accusations and attacks.

Example: A believer filled with peace and joy becomes a strong witness in hostile environments.

Practical Insight

- Pursue holiness and surrender daily to allow the Spirit to bear fruit in your life.

- Use the fruit of the Spirit to build up others and defuse conflict.

Key Memory Verses

- John 14:26

- Romans 8:26

- Ephesians 5:18

- Galatians 5:22–23

Reflection Questions

- How are you relying on the Holy Spirit in your spiritual battles?

- In what areas do you need to cultivate greater sensitivity and dependence on His guidance and power?

....

....

....

....

- Why is the Holy Spirit essential in spiritual warfare rather than optional?

....

....

....

....

- In what ways does the presence of the Holy Spirit provide both comfort and a catalyst for bold action?

....

....

....

....

How does the fruit of the Spirit transform your inner life to help you overcome outward battles?

....

....

....

....

....

Exercises

1. **Holy Spirit Journal**: Spend ten minutes each day this week journaling anything the Holy Spirit reveals to you through prayer or Scripture.

2. **Fruit Assessment**: Choose one fruit of the Spirit to focus on each day for a week. Ask God to grow that fruit in your life through situations that stretch your faith.

3. **Intercession Practice**: Spend time praying in the Spirit or asking the Spirit to intercede through you for a specific need.

Discussion Questions

- How have you experienced the Holy Spirit's guidance in difficult situations?

- Why is the fruit of the Spirit vital to spiritual warfare?

- What is the difference between fighting in your strength versus His strength?

Prayer Guide

Prayer for Filling, Guidance, and Victory: "Holy Spirit, I welcome You into every part of my life. Fill me afresh today with Your power and peace. Lead me into truth, teach me to pray, and grow Your fruit in me. I choose to rely on Your strength, not my own, as I walk in victory. In Jesus's name, Amen."

Prayer for Gifts and Spiritual Refinement: "Holy Spirit, stir up and refine the gifts You've placed in me for Your glory."

Topics Covered

- Empowerment for battle

- Guidance and wisdom

- Intercession on our behalf

- Filling with the fruit of the Spirit

Chapter 24:
Spiritual Warfare and the Church Body

Key Scriptures

- *Ephesians 4:11–13—"So Christ himself gave the apostles, the prophets, the evangelists, the pastors and teachers, to equip his people for works of service, so that the body of Christ may be built up until we all reach unity in the faith and in the knowledge of the Son of God and become mature, attaining to the whole measure of the fullness of Christ."*

- *Matthew 18:20—"For where two or three gather in my name, there am I with them."*

- *Acts 4:31—"After they prayed, the place where they were meeting was shaken. And they were all filled with the Holy Spirit and spoke the word of God boldly."*

Overview

Spiritual warfare is not just an individual battle. It is deeply connected to the life and health of the Church body. The Church as a community of believers is called to stand together in unity, prayer, and mutual support to combat the enemy's schemes. This chapter explores how corporate spiritual warfare operates, the importance of unity, and the role of church leadership in equipping the Body for victory.

Expanded Study

1. The Power of Corporate Prayer and Worship

When believers gather in unity, there is spiritual power that can't be matched individually. Jesus said where two or three gather in His name, He is present (Matthew 18:20).

Examples

- The early Church in Acts 4 prayed corporately, and God answered by filling them with boldness.

- Corporate worship shifts spiritual atmospheres, breaking chains and inviting God's presence.

Practical Insight

- Participate actively in church prayer meetings and worship gatherings.

- Organize or join spiritual warfare prayer teams.

2. Unity as a Defensive and Offensive Strategy

Unity protects the church from division, which Satan often uses as a weapon (1 Corinthians 1:10). A unified Church body is a strong fortress against spiritual attacks.

Example: Jesus prayed for unity among His disciples (John 17:20–23), knowing this would strengthen their witness and resistance to the enemy.

Practical Insight

- Pursue reconciliation and forgiveness in relationships.

- Promote a culture of humility and service within the church.

3. The Role of Leadership in Equipping the Church

Pastors, elders, and ministry leaders have the responsibility to train and equip believers in spiritual warfare (Ephesians 4:11–13).

Responsibilities

- Teaching biblical truth about spiritual battles

- Providing practical tools like prayer models and warfare strategies

- Encouraging accountability and mentoring

Example: A church that regularly teaches on spiritual warfare and organizes prayer ministries often sees breakthroughs in personal and community challenges.

---

4. Spiritual Gifts and Ministries in Corporate Warfare

Each believer's gifts contribute to the Body's strength in warfare. Gifts like intercession, prophecy, healing, and discernment help the Church stand firm.

Practical Insight

- Identify and activate your gifts for the Church's benefit.

- Support ministries focused on deliverance, healing, and prayer.

Example: A prophecy team in a local church regularly prays for the congregation, bringing encouragement and direction that dismantle spiritual strongholds.

---

5. Building a Culture of Spiritual Alertness

Churches that thrive in spiritual warfare foster vigilance and preparedness.

Practical Suggestions

- Incorporate spiritual warfare teachings in sermons and small groups.

- Encourage members to put on the full armor of God daily.

- Create environments where believers can share testimonies and prayer requests safely.

Key Memory Verses

- Ephesians 4:11–13

- Matthew 18:20

- John 17:20–23

- 1 Corinthians 1:10

Reflection Questions

- How does your church body engage in spiritual warfare?

....

....

....

....

- Are you actively contributing your gifts and prayers for the health of the community?

....

....

....

- What steps can your church take to grow stronger in unity and spiritual vigilance?

....

....

....

● How does corporate intercession invite corporate breakthrough within the Church?

....

....

....

....

● Why is it important for the Church to move from being passive spectators to active spiritual warriors?

....

....

....

....

● In what ways should leadership equip, not just encourage, the Body of Christ?

....

....

....

....

Exercises

1. **Church Intercession Night**: Attend or organize a group prayer meeting focused on spiritual warfare and intercession for your city.

2. **Unity Action Plan**: Identify a past or present conflict in your church or ministry. Take one step toward healing or strengthening unity this week.

3. **Gift Collaboration**: Partner with someone in your church who has a different spiritual gift than you. Pray or minister together.

Discussion Questions

- How has corporate prayer impacted your spiritual life?

- In what ways can your local church become more spiritually alert?

- What is your role in corporate spiritual warfare?

Prayer Guide

"Lord, raise up Your Church as a mighty army. Unite our hearts in love, truth, and purpose. Let our worship be warfare and our prayers be powerful. Equip our leaders and members to stand firm and move forward together. Make us bold, Spirit-filled, and ready for battle. In Jesus's name, Amen."

Topics Covered:

- The power of corporate prayer and worship

- Unity as a defensive and offensive strategy

- The role of leadership in equipping the Church

- Spiritual gifts and ministries in corporate warfare

- Building a culture of spiritual alertness

Chapter 25:
Overcoming Spiritual Fatigue

Key Scriptures

- *Matthew 11:28–30—"Come to me, all you who are weary and burdened, and I will give you rest. Take my yoke upon you and learn from me, for I am gentle and humble in heart, and you will find rest for your souls."*

- *Psalm 23:1–3—"He restores my soul. He leads me in paths of righteousness for his name's sake."*

- *Isaiah 40:29–31—"He gives strength to the weary and increases the power of the weak. Those who hope in the Lord will renew their strength. They will soar on wings like eagles; they will run and not grow weary, they will walk and not be faint."*

- *Exodus 33:14—"My presence will go with you, and I will give you rest."*

Overview

Spiritual warfare can be exhausting, leaving believers feeling drained, discouraged, or disconnected from God. Spiritual fatigue is a natural reality, especially during prolonged struggles. This chapter focuses on **recognizing spiritual weariness, understanding its causes, and applying practical biblical strategies to restore strength and renewal**. By intentionally seeking God's presence, practicing restorative spiritual disciplines, and nurturing the soul, believers can regain vitality and be prepared for future battles.

Expanded Study

1. Recognizing Spiritual Fatigue

Spiritual fatigue may show up as emotional burnout, loss of joy, reduced prayer life, or a sense of defeat. Signs include:

- Feeling overwhelmed by daily spiritual disciplines

- Loss of motivation for prayer, worship, or ministry

- Doubting God's presence or effectiveness
  Example: A believer prayed faithfully for years without visible breakthrough and began to feel spiritually empty and discouraged.

2. Root Causes of Weariness

Identifying the causes helps in addressing fatigue effectively:

- **Isolation:** Facing battles alone can drain strength.

- **Unresolved Sin:** Guilt and shame weigh heavily on the spirit.

- **Neglect of Rest:** Physical and spiritual rest is essential for renewal.

- **Discouragement from Delayed Answers:** Waiting for God's timing can feel exhausting.

Practical Insight:

- Regularly confess and repent of hidden sins.

- Build supportive community connections.

- Prioritize Sabbath and restorative practices.

3. Biblical Examples of Restoration

The Bible shows how God restores weary believers:

- **Elijah:** Exhausted and discouraged, God renewed him with food, water, and rest (1 Kings 19:1–8).

- **David:** Expressed weariness and sought God's renewal through prayer and worship (Psalm 42:1–5).

- **Jesus:** Withdrew for prayer and rest even in the midst of ministry and trials (Luke 5:16).

Practical Insight: Reflect on these examples and journal how God has restored you in past struggles.

---

4. Strategies for Renewal

- **Daily Dependence on God:** Begin each day seeking the Holy Spirit's guidance and strength (Isaiah 40:31).

- **Prayer and Worship:** Refresh the soul through focused prayer and worship music.

- **Scripture Meditation:** Memorize passages that bring peace, hope, and encouragement.

- **Community Encouragement:** Share struggles and receive prayer and counsel from trusted believers.

- **Physical Care:** Attend to sleep, nutrition, and light exercise to support spiritual and physical vitality.
  Example: A woman instituted a morning routine of Scripture reading, worship, and a short walk, which renewed her spirit and energy.

---

5. Living in God's Sustaining Presence

- Trust God's presence to restore strength daily.

- Recognize that brief times of rest and reflection with Him strengthen for future battles.

- Isaiah 40:31 reminds us that those who wait on the Lord **renew their strength and soar like eagles**.

Reflection Questions

- What areas of your spiritual life feel most drained?

- Which practices help you feel restored and connected to God?

- How can you incorporate intentional rest and renewal into your daily life?

Exercises

1. **Fatigue Inventory:** List symptoms of spiritual fatigue you are experiencing. Identify one practical step to address them this week.

2. **Rest and Refuel Plan:** Design a "Sabbath Day" or mini-retreat within the next thirty days including Scripture reading, worship, rest, and silence.

3. **Renewal Journal:** Each day for a week, write down ways God refreshed your spirit or answered prayers, even in small ways.

Discussion Questions

- How do you recognize spiritual fatigue in yourself or others?

- How can rest and restoration be used strategically in spiritual warfare?

- Who can you reach out to for accountability and encouragement when weary?

Prayer Guide

Prayer for Refreshment and Spiritual Renewal: "Lord, I confess my weariness and ask for Your renewing strength. Restore my soul, revive my spirit, and guide me in Your presence. Help me take intentional time to rest in You, trusting that even brief moments of reflection and prayer renew me for Your work. Amen."

Topics Covered

- Recognizing spiritual fatigue

- Root causes of weariness

- Biblical examples of restoration

- Strategies for renewal

- Living in God's sustaining presence

Chapter 26:
Victory in Christ—Living as Overcomers

Key Scriptures

- *1 John 5:4–5—"For everyone born of God overcomes the world. This is the victory that has overcome the world, even our faith. Who is it that overcomes the world? Only the one who believes that Jesus is the Son of God."*

- *Romans 8:37—"No, in all these things we are more than conquerors through him who loved us."*

Overview

The ultimate victory in spiritual warfare is found in Jesus Christ. Believers are not merely called to survive the battles; we are called to thrive as overcomers, embodying the authority, freedom, and power bestowed upon us through Christ. Our identity as overcomers is firmly rooted in the finished work of Christ on the cross. Victory is not a distant aspiration. It is a present reality that we can experience daily.

As we learn to walk in this truth, we equip ourselves to overcome spiritual attacks and, in turn, empower others to do the same. This chapter emphasizes the importance of embracing our identity in Christ, consistently living in victory, and actively encouraging our fellow believers to stand firm in their faith. By recognizing who we are in Him, we can navigate life's challenges with confidence and strength, knowing that we are more than conquerors through Him who loves us.

Expanded Study

1. Understanding Our Identity as Overcomers

As born-again believers, our position is secure in Christ. We are no longer slaves to sin, fear, or the enemy's lies.

Key Truths

- We are children of God, loved and accepted (John 1:12).

- We have been given authority over all the power of the enemy (Luke 10:19).

- Victory is not based on our strength but on Christ's finished work.

Example: A believer struggling with condemnation was reminded of Romans 8:1—*"There is therefore now no condemnation for those who are in Christ Jesus"*—which changed her mindset and strengthened her faith.

---

2. Living Daily in Victory

Victory is a daily choice to stand firm, resist the enemy, and walk in obedience.

Practices to Maintain Victory

- Regular prayer and reliance on the Holy Spirit

- Speaking God's Word boldly against lies and fear

- Maintaining a lifestyle of holiness and repentance

Example: A man dealing with temptation committed to daily confession and Scripture declaration, leading to lasting freedom.

---

3. Overcoming Through Faith

Faith is the key to accessing victory.

Hebrews 11:1—"Now faith is confidence in what we hope for and assurance about what we do not see."

Practical Insight

- Trust God's promises even when circumstances look bleak.

- Remember testimonies of God's faithfulness to build confidence.

4. Encouraging Others to Stand Firm

Victory is not just personal; it is communal.

Encouragement

- Sharing testimonies of God's deliverance

- Praying with and for fellow believers

- Mentoring new believers in their walk of faith

Example: A small group regularly shares breakthroughs in prayer, encouraging one another to persevere.

5. The Eternal Perspective

Our ultimate victory will be fully realized when Christ returns.

Encouragement

- Keep your eyes on the eternal reward (Revelation 21:7).

- Live with hope and expectancy.

Key Memory Verses

- 1 John 5:4–5

- Romans 8:37

- Luke 10:19

- Hebrews 11:1

Reflection Questions

- Do you fully embrace your identity as an overcomer in Christ?

- How can you walk more confidently in daily victory?

- In what ways can you encourage others in their battles?

- What does it mean to fight from victory rather than fight for it?

- How does your faith determine your focus in spiritual or personal battles?

....

....

....

....

....

- In what ways is helping others win part of your calling as an overcomer?

....

....

....

....

....

Exercises

1. **Victory Journal**: Write a testimony of a time you overcame a difficult situation by faith. Revisit it during hard times.

2. **Encouragement Outreach**: Choose someone who is in a spiritual battle. Write them a note, text, or call to encourage them with Scripture.

3. **Faith Declarations**: Write and speak daily faith declarations that affirm your identity in Christ and His promises.

Discussion Questions

- What does it practically mean to be an overcomer?

- How does faith help you maintain a victorious perspective?

- In what ways can you help others walk in victory?

Prayer Guide

"Father, thank You that in Christ I am an overcomer. Help me to walk daily in that truth and not be swayed by circumstances. Strengthen my faith, renew my mind, and use me to encourage others. Give me an eternal perspective that lifts me above every battle. In Jesus's name, Amen."

Topics Covered

- Understanding our identity as overcomers

- Living daily in victory

- Overcoming through faith

- Encouraging others to stand firm

- The eternal perspective

Chapter 27:
The Role of the Church in Spiritual Warfare

Key Scriptures

- *Ephesians 6:12—"For our struggle is not against flesh and blood, but against the rulers, against the authorities, against the powers of this dark world and against the spiritual forces of evil in the heavenly realms."*

- *Matthew 18:19–20—"Again, truly I tell you that if two of you on earth agree about anything they ask for, it will be done for them by my Father in heaven. For where two or three gather in my name, there am I with them."*

Overview

Spiritual warfare is a significant aspect of our faith that transcends individual struggles; it's a collective endeavor that highlights the role of the Church as the Body of Christ. When believers unite in purpose, love, and prayer, they tap into a powerful synergy against the enemy. The effectiveness of this corporate battle relies on key elements like agreement, discernment, and the activation of spiritual gifts within the community.

Division, in contrast, weakens our ability to confront challenges, while unity can amplify our spiritual effectiveness and impact. This chapter delves into how fostering unity, engaging in prayer, and practicing intercession collectively empowers believers to face darkness more effectively, illustrating the strength found in togetherness as we stand firm in faith.

By embracing this corporate approach to spiritual warfare, we not only fortify the Church but also create an environment that nurtures growth, accountability, and victory in Christ.

Expanded Study

1. Understanding Corporate Spiritual Warfare

The enemy often targets the Church to disrupt God's purposes. Spiritual battles fought in unity are more powerful than those fought alone.

Biblical Examples

- The early Church in Acts gathered continually in prayer, resulting in boldness and miracles (Acts 4:31).

- The walls of Jerusalem fell when the people prayed and fasted together (Nehemiah 4:9).

Practical Insight

- Seek unity and reconciliation within your local church body.

- Engage in corporate prayer and fasting for spiritual breakthroughs.

2. The Power of Agreement

Jesus promises that when believers agree in prayer, powerful results follow.

Key Points

- Agreement releases spiritual authority.

- Collective faith can break strongholds and bring revival.

Example: A prayer team consistently agreed in prayer over a community plagued by violence. Over time, crime rates dropped, and lives were transformed.

3. Intercession as a Corporate Weapon

Intercessory prayer involves standing in the gap for others and for the church community.

How to Develop Corporate Intercession

- Organize prayer groups focusing on spiritual warfare.

- Use Scripture-based prayers to declare God's promises over your city or church.

- Train members in spiritual discernment to pray effectively.

---

4. Spiritual Gifts and Ministries in the Church Body

Every believer contributes to spiritual warfare through their gifts and ministries.

Key Gifts in Corporate Warfare

- Prophecy to expose lies and guide direction

- Healing to restore and strengthen the body

- Deliverance ministries to set captives free

Practical Insight

- Encourage and support diverse ministries in your church.

- Serve together to build a strong spiritual community.

---

5. Resisting Division and Strengthening Unity

Division weakens the Church and opens doors to the enemy.

Strategies to Promote Unity

- Practice humility and forgiveness.

- Focus on common goals and mission.

- Celebrate diversity within the Body.

Example: A divided congregation experienced increased strife and spiritual attacks until they committed to reconciliation and unity, after which peace and growth followed.

Key Memory Verses

- Ephesians 6:12

- Matthew 18:19–20

- Acts 4:31

- Nehemiah 4:9

Reflection Questions

- How actively do you participate in your church's spiritual warfare efforts?

- What role can you take to promote unity and corporate prayer?

- How can your gifts serve the Body in these battles?

- How does unity in prayer bring exponential spiritual power?

- In what ways does God work mightily when the Church prays and acts as one?

- Why does disunity disrupt destiny, and how can you guard your heart and relationships?

....

....

....

....

....

Exercises:

1. **Unity Audit**: Reflect on any unresolved conflict or division within your church or ministry circle. Ask God for wisdom and take one step toward reconciliation.

2. **Intercession Group**: Join or form a prayer group committed to weekly intercession for your church, city, or nation.

3. **Gift Activation**: Identify your spiritual gift(s) and one way you can use them within your local church this month to strengthen others.

Discussion Questions

- What role does unity play in effective spiritual warfare?

- How can the local church improve in corporate intercession?

- What are some ways to overcome division within the Church?

Prayer Guide

Prayer for Church Unity and Spiritual Alignment: "Father, unify Your Church under the banner of Christ. Teach us to war together in love and truth. Let agreement be our strength, and let Your Spirit guide our prayers and actions. Heal any division and empower us with boldness to advance Your Kingdom together. In Jesus's name, Amen."

Topics Covered

- Understanding corporate spiritual warfare

- The power of agreement

- Intercession as a corporate weapon

- Spiritual gifts and ministries in the Church Body

- Resisting division and strengthening unity

Chapter 28: Perseverance and Hope in Spiritual Warfare

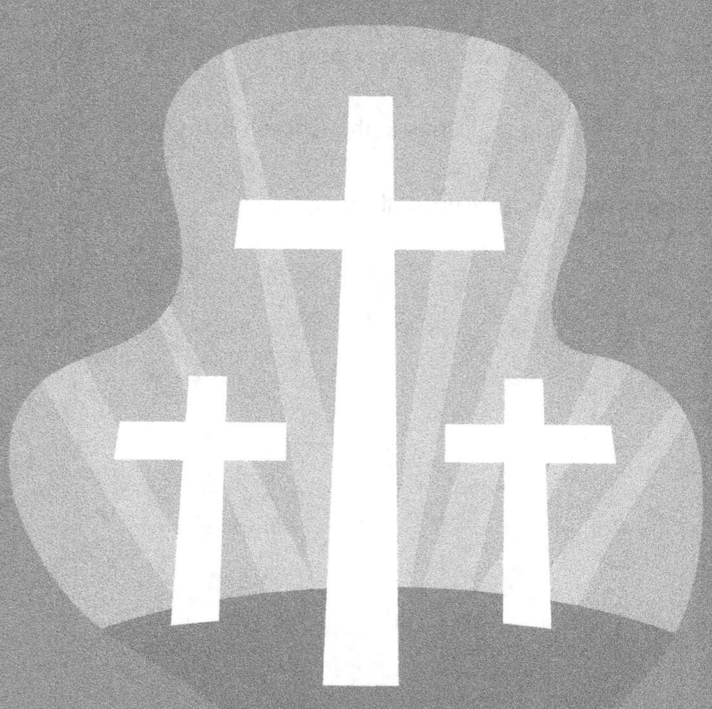

Key Scriptures

- *James 1:12—"Blessed is the one who perseveres under trial because, having stood the test, that person will receive the crown of life that the Lord has promised to those who love him."*

- *Romans 12:12—"Be joyful in hope, patient in affliction, faithful in prayer."*

- *Hebrews 10:36—"You need to persevere so that when you have done the will of God, you will receive what he has promised."*

Overview

Spiritual warfare is indeed a challenging and prolonged journey, reminding us that it often requires significant endurance and perseverance. Just as in a marathon, we must be committed for the long haul, continuously seeking strength and hope in the midst of trials and setbacks. It's essential for us, as soldiers of Christ, to remain steadfast and faithful, trusting in the promises God has made to us.

This chapter emphasizes the importance of nurturing perseverance and hope based on His Word. By holding on to these promises, we can develop spiritual resilience, which enables us to face difficulties with confidence. Ultimately, we can be assured of the victory that comes through Christ, knowing that our struggles are not in vain.

In this light, we can encourage one another to stay focused on the finish line, reminding ourselves of the great reward that awaits those who uphold their faith in the face of adversity. Let's continue to cultivate our endurance, nurture our hope, and trust in God's unwavering promises as we navigate through the battles ahead.

Expanded Study

1. The Necessity of Perseverance

Spiritual battles may last for days, months, or even years. Perseverance means continuing to stand firm despite difficulties.

Biblical Examples

- Job's endurance through immense suffering (Job 1–2).

- Paul's multiple imprisonments and hardships (2 Corinthians 11:23–28).

Practical Insight

- Recognize that perseverance refines faith and character.

- Celebrate small victories to stay motivated.

2. Hope as an Anchor

Hope sustains believers by focusing on God's promises rather than present circumstances.

Hebrews 6:19—"We have this hope as an anchor for the soul, firm and secure."

Practical Tips

- Meditate regularly on God's promises of deliverance.

- Use worship and praise to lift your spirit during hard times.

3. Faithfulness in Prayer

Consistent prayer is vital for endurance in spiritual warfare.

Tips for Maintaining Prayer Life

- Set regular prayer times—even short but frequent moments.

- Use Scripture as a foundation for prayers.

- Join prayer partners or groups for mutual encouragement.

---

4. Overcoming Discouragement and Burnout

Discouragement can be a tactic of the enemy to cause believers to give up.

Strategies

- Stay connected to community for support.

- Take spiritual and physical rest when needed.

- Remind yourself of past victories and God's faithfulness.

Example: A woman felt overwhelmed by spiritual attacks until a mentor encouraged her to rest and remember God's past deliverances in her life.

---

5. Looking Toward the Eternal Reward

Understanding that our present struggles are temporary helps believers persevere.

2 Corinthians 4:17–18—"For our light and momentary troubles are achieving for us an eternal glory that far outweighs them all."

Encouragement

- Fix your eyes on the eternal prize.

- Live with hope and expectancy for Christ's return.

Key Memory Verses

- James 1:12

- Romans 12:12

- Hebrews 6:19

- 2 Corinthians 4:17–18

Reflection Questions

- How do you respond when spiritual battles feel long or difficult?

- What practical steps can you take to cultivate perseverance and hope today?

How can you encourage others who are weary in the fight? Discouragement is natural but not final—God gives grace for each day.

How is endurance built one step at a time through spiritual habits and hope?

In what ways does an eternal perspective change how we approach today's battles?

Exercises

1. **Hope Reminder**: Write down five promises of God that give you hope. Keep them in a visible place this week.

2. **Prayer Consistency Plan**: Choose a specific time each day to pray for endurance and strength. Track your consistency for seven days.

3. **Eternal Perspective Journal**: Reflect on how your current spiritual battle might look different in light of eternity. What would you say to yourself ten years from now about today's struggle?

Discussion Questions

- What has helped you persevere in difficult seasons?

- How can the Church encourage long-term faithfulness?

- What role does the eternal reward play in daily decisions?

Prayer Guide

"Lord, strengthen me to press on when I feel weak. Let hope rise in my heart and faithfulness mark my journey. Teach me to persevere in prayer and walk with endurance, looking always to the joy set before me. Help me to live with eternity in mind and not give up. In Jesus's name, Amen.

Topics Covered

- The necessity of perseverance

- Hope as an anchor

- Faithfulness in prayer

- Overcoming discouragement and burnout

- Looking toward the eternal reward

Chapter 29:
The Victory of Christ and Our Position in Him

Key Scriptures

- *Colossians 2:15—"And having disarmed the powers and authorities, He made a public spectacle of them, triumphing over them by the cross."*

- *1 Corinthians 15:57—"But thanks be to God! He gives us the victory through our Lord Jesus Christ."*

Overview

The foundation of every believer's victory in spiritual warfare is the finished work of Jesus Christ on the cross. Spiritual warfare concludes in victory because Christ has already triumphed over every obstacle. Our strength is rooted in grasping and aligning with the truth of what Christ accomplished through His sacrifice. This chapter delves into the importance of Christ's victory over sin, death, and demonic forces, highlighting how recognizing our identity and position in Him equips us to engage with authority and confidence.

Expanded Study

1. Christ's Triumph Over the Enemy

Jesus's death and resurrection were decisive defeats over Satan and all spiritual forces opposed to God's Kingdom.

- **Colossians 2:15** reveals that Jesus disarmed the rulers and authorities.

- The cross is not only a symbol of sacrifice but a declaration of victory.

Example: The resurrection transformed the despair of the disciples into bold proclamation of the Gospel, defeating fear and death.

2. Our Position "In Christ"

Believers are united with Christ in His victory.

- **Romans 6:6–7** speaks of being crucified with Christ so that the power of sin is broken.

- **Ephesians 2:6** declares that believers are seated with Christ in heavenly places.

Practical Insight

- Walk daily remembering your authority as one seated with Christ.

- Stand firm in the truth that sin and the enemy have been defeated on your behalf.

3. Walking in Authority and Confidence

Knowing Christ's victory should lead to boldness in spiritual battles.

- Use the name of Jesus confidently (Philippians 2:9–11).

- Declare Scripture boldly as your authority (Luke 10:19).

Example: Early believers faced persecution with courage because they understood their victory was secured in Christ.

4. Living From Victory, Not Victimhood

It is essential to reject a mindset of defeat and embrace identity as an overcomer.

- *1 John 5:4–5—"Everyone born of God overcomes the world."*

- Victory is not about never facing trials but about prevailing through Christ.

Practical Exercise

- Write down key victory Scriptures and meditate on them daily.

- Replace negative or fearful thoughts with truths about your position in Christ.

5. The Future Glory and Ultimate Defeat of Evil

While victory is already won, believers look forward to Christ's final return when evil will be fully eradicated.

- **Revelation 20:10** describes the ultimate defeat of Satan.

- This hope strengthens believers to persevere.

Key Memory Verses

- Colossians 2:15

- 1 Corinthians 15:57

- Romans 6:6–7

- Ephesians 2:6

Reflection Questions

- How does understanding Christ's victory impact your confidence in spiritual warfare?

- Are you living daily from a place of victory or victimhood?

- How can you encourage others to embrace their identity "in Christ"?

- How does knowing that Jesus has already won every battle affect the way you face challenges?

....

....

....

....

- In what ways does your authority come from your position in Christ rather than your own strength?

....

....

....

....

- How can your daily walk reflect the confidence that comes from Christ's finished work?

....

....

....

....

Exercises

1. **Victory Identity Statements**: Write three declarations about your authority and identity in Christ. Say them daily.

2. **Scripture Mapping**: Study Colossians 2:13–15 and list every action Christ took on your behalf. Meditate on them.

3. **Victory Perspective Check**: Journal where you have been living from a mindset of defeat. Replace it with truth from Scripture.

Discussion Questions

- What does it mean to be "seated with Christ"?

- How can we move from a mindset of victimhood to victory?

- How should Christ's ultimate victory influence how we engage in spiritual warfare today?

Prayer Guide

"Jesus, thank You for defeating the enemy and setting me free. Help me live boldly from the victory of the cross. Remove any victim mindset from my life and fill me with courage, faith, and heavenly perspective. Let me walk in Your authority, knowing You have triumphed forever. In Your name I pray, Amen."

Topics Covered

- Christ's triumph over the enemy

- Our position "in Christ"

- Walking in authority and confidence

- Living from victory, not victimhood

- The future glory and ultimate defeat of evil

Chapter 30: Equipping the Next Generation for Spiritual Warfare

Key Scriptures

- *2 Timothy 2:2—"And the things you have heard me say in the presence of many witnesses entrust to reliable people who will also be qualified to teach others."*

- *Deuteronomy 6:6–7—"These commandments that I give you today are to be on your hearts. Impress them on your children. Talk about them when you sit at home and when you walk along the road..."*

Overview

Spiritual warfare extends beyond our individual journeys; we must take on the responsibility of discipling and mentoring others, especially the next generation, helping them to remain steadfast in the Lord and adhere to truth. Passing on the knowledge, tools, and spiritual practices needed for effective spiritual warfare is essential for the health and growth of the Church. By focusing on mentoring, teaching, and empowering younger believers, we can cultivate a lasting legacy of faith, courage, and victory. This chapter emphasizes the significance of generational transfer, establishing strong foundations in faith early on, nurturing boldness, and fostering a supportive culture that promotes spiritual resilience.

Expanded Study

1. The Importance of Mentoring and Discipleship

Spiritual warfare skills are best learned in community through example, teaching, and practice.

- Paul's mentorship of Timothy highlights the value of intentional training.

- Mentors provide wisdom, encouragement, and accountability.

Practical Insight

- Seek out mentors who walk in spiritual maturity.

- If you are mature, invest in younger believers with patience and love.

2. Teaching Biblical Foundations Early

Grounding young believers in Scripture and spiritual realities prevents deception.

- Teach the Armor of God (Ephesians 6) as a daily practice.

- Encourage knowledge of God's promises and the power of prayer.

Example: A youth leader incorporates Scripture memorization and prayer exercises in weekly meetings, building confidence and spiritual sensitivity in teens.

3. Encouraging Boldness and Faith

The next generation must learn to stand firm and fight with confidence.

- Share testimonies of victory to inspire courage.

- Create safe spaces for young people to step out in faith and spiritual gifts.

Practical Tip

- Encourage youth to pray aloud, engage in intercession, and practice discernment.

4. Navigating Modern Challenges

Today's young believers face unique challenges including digital distractions, spiritual relativism, and cultural pressure.

- Teach discernment about media and peer influence.

- Equip them with practical tools for daily spiritual battle.

Example: A mentor guides young adults in setting boundaries on social media and using prayer apps to stay connected with God.

5. Building a Culture of Support and Accountability

Community and peer support are crucial for sustaining spiritual health.

- Promote small groups, prayer teams, and accountability partnerships.

- Encourage confession, encouragement, and mutual prayer.

Scriptural Model: Ecclesiastes 4:9–12 highlights the strength found in companionship.

Key Memory Verses

- 2 Timothy 2:2

- Deuteronomy 6:6–7

- Ephesians 6:10–18

- Ecclesiastes 4:9–12

Reflection Questions

- Are you actively involved in mentoring or being mentored?

- How can you contribute to equipping others for spiritual warfare?

....

....

....

- What steps can you take to foster faith and boldness in the next generation?

....

....

....

- How are you called to pass on what God has taught you to others?

....

....

....

- Why is discipleship both intentional and relational?

....

....

....

In what ways does it take a community to raise spiritually mature believers?

....

....

....

....

....

Exercises

1. **Mentorship Mapping**

    o   List three people in your life who have mentored or influenced your spiritual walk.

    o   Identify one person you could mentor or encourage in spiritual warfare.

    o   Write down one practical step you can take this week to connect with that person.

2. **Armor of God Memorization**

    o   Memorize Ephesians 6:10–18 over the next week.

    o   Each day, focus on one piece of the armor, reflecting on its meaning and how it applies to your life.

3. **Media and Distraction Audit**

    ○   Keep a journal for three days tracking your media consumption (social media, TV, music).

    ○   Identify any content that may weaken your spiritual focus.

    ○   Create a personal plan to replace that time with prayer, Scripture, or worship.

4. **Boldness Practice**

    ○   Find a trusted friend or group and practice praying out loud, sharing a brief testimony, or speaking a Scripture declaration.

    ○   Reflect on how it felt to step out in faith and what you learned.

5. **Culture Builder**: Reflect on how your church or family environment can better support spiritual growth for the next generation.

Discussion Questions:

1. Why is mentoring important in spiritual warfare? How can it impact both the mentor and mentee?

2. What are some challenges young believers face today in their spiritual battles?

3. How can we create safe environments for youth and new believers to practice their faith boldly?

4. In what ways can we encourage each other to stay vigilant and strong in prayer and Scripture?

5. How does memorizing Scripture empower you in spiritual warfare?

Prayer Guide

- **For Mentors and Leaders:**
  "Lord, raise up mentors and spiritual leaders who will faithfully guide the next generation in truth and boldness. Give them wisdom, patience, and love."

- **For the Next Generation:**
  "Father, strengthen young believers with Your Spirit. Help them to know their identity in Christ, stand firm against the enemy, and walk in boldness and faith."

- **For Protection and Discernment:**
  "Jesus, guard the hearts and minds of the youth. Help them discern truth from lies and avoid distractions that weaken their walk with You."

- **For Courage to Step Out:**
  "Holy Spirit, fill us with courage to pray aloud, share our testimonies, and use the gifts You have given us for Your glory."

- **For Unity and Accountability:**
  "God, build strong communities where believers encourage, support, and hold one another accountable in love."

- "Father, thank You for entrusting me with the call to disciple others. Give me wisdom, patience, and love to guide those around me into deeper truth and freedom. Help me to model boldness and faith and to raise up leaders who will multiply for Your Kingdom. In Jesus's name, Amen."

Topics Covered

- The importance of mentoring and discipleship

- Teaching biblical foundations early

- Encouraging boldness and faith

- Navigating modern challenges

- Building a culture of support and accountability

My Testimony

My life was going great. I met my husband, and we got married. However, after the birth of our fourth child, I became ill. Initially, I thought it was something normal—something that just happens—yet deep down, I sensed it wasn't. Outwardly, everything seemed normal, but I had unknowingly stepped into a spiritual warfare I was not prepared for.

For nearly eight years, I suffered. I couldn't work, and I lived in deep pain—physically, emotionally, and spiritually. But even during my darkest moments, the Lord provided for me and my family. When I realized this was not merely a health issue but a spiritual battle, I began to seek God more fervently.

I grew up in a Christian household, and my mother faithfully took my siblings and me to church, not just on Sundays but to various services, especially fasting services. My late father led us in nightly devotions. I believed I was serving God wholeheartedly, yet I later recognized that there were open doors in my life through which the enemy gained access. People who were unaware of my struggles targeted me for their selfish and even evil ambitions.

A few months after my injury, the Lord prompted me to start a prayer line. As I drew closer to God, prayed more, read my Bible more, and fasted regularly, my life began to shift. One day, a friend called to inform me about a PhD program he thought I could benefit from. Despite my health challenges, I felt compelled to pursue it. I took out a loan and enrolled in classes. The journey was difficult.

Before starting the PhD program, I had two surgeries—one on my knee and one on my shoulder. The shoulder surgery caused nerve pain in my hand, which was later diagnosed as carpal tunnel. The hand specialist recommended surgery, I declined. I was also told I needed back surgery, which I also refused. Even with online classes, I struggled to sit long enough to complete assignments. Most of the time, I worked while lying on my back with my computer on a pillow.

Returning to school became a family project, and it was incredibly challenging. There were many days I cried and wanted to give up. Yet, God surrounded me with people who had walked similar paths and faithful prayer warriors who encouraged me to keep going.

On June 15, 2023, I visited my back doctor at UM with my husband, who told me, "There's nothing else we can do. You just have to learn to live with the pain." That day, I realized this wasn't just a medical battle; it was a God battle.

That very day, I decided I was going back to work. Although still in pain, I had a dream where I understood God was telling me, "Go back to work, and I will heal you." I clung to that promise and walked in obedience.

August is the month of **restoration and restitution**, and so I began applying for teaching positions. Since I hadn't been in the classroom for years, I accepted a substitute job to test my strength. The pain was so intense, I thought it would break me. I cried constantly, yet I pressed on.

On the third day of subbing, a friend called and said, "I had a dream about you. You were collecting hay."

I immediately understood: It was harvest time. I stopped going to the school that I was subbing at and waited on God.

Soon after, another friend mentioned a sister in my church was asking for me, stating that a job was forthcoming. The following Saturday, I received an email from a school informing me I had been hired. I accepted the position because God had spoken, and as a child of God, that's all you need.

The first year was tough. Knowing the enemy aimed to destroy me, I stood firm in prayer. The enemy tried every tactic to make me lose everything, but my faithful God, the One who never fails, saved me.

Every day, I cried on my way to and from work. When I returned home, I couldn't even make it to my bedroom; I had to lie on the couch instead. I relied on strong medications just to make it through the day. Still, God provided. The school assigned a paraprofessional to assist me, and my kindness inspired her to share how I treated her with compassion to others.

As she spread the word, more people came forward to help. Kindness goes a long way!

In August 2024, I proudly earned my doctoral degree from St. Thomas University. Just like Joseph's words in Genesis 50:20 remind us: *"You intended to harm me, but God intended it for good to accomplish what is now being done, the saving of many lives."*

God transformed my pain, setbacks, and struggles into something good.

As I conclude, I want to leave you with this final encouragement: Life isn't always easy. You will face setbacks. You'll encounter people who may dislike you for no reason and others who might try to hurt you.

But remember: You are God's child. Stay focused. You are never too young to serve God, nor too safe from the enemy's attacks. This is why you must be spiritually prepared.

Read your Bible. Pray daily. Stay committed to your walk with Christ.

The battle is real, **spiritual warfare is very real**, but so **is the victory found in Jesus Christ**. **Do not compromise.** Serve God wholeheartedly.

I guarantee you, by the Word of God and personal experience, you will live a **victorious life in Christ**.

—Dr. Rosemica D. Bonhomme

Conclusion: Walking Forward in Victory

As you reach the end of this workbook, remember that spiritual warfare is not a season you visit; it is a reality of the Christian life. Yet it is not a reality meant to produce fear, confusion, or defeat. Through Jesus Christ, the victory has already been won.

Throughout these chapters, you have learned that the battle is real, the enemy is limited, and your authority in Christ is secure. You have explored the power of God's Word, the strength of prayer and fasting, the covering of worship, the protection of the armor of God, and the importance of community and discernment. These are not abstract ideas, but practical tools meant to be used daily as you walk with God.

Spiritual warfare is not about striving harder; it is about standing firmer. You do not fight to gain victory; you fight from the victory Christ secured on the cross. As a son or daughter of God, you are called to live alert, anchored in truth, clothed in righteousness, and empowered by the Holy Spirit.

May this workbook serve not as an ending, but as a beginning; a catalyst for deeper intimacy with God, greater spiritual awareness, and a lifestyle marked by freedom, courage, and perseverance. When challenges arise, return to these truths. When the battle intensifies, remember who you are and whose you are.

Go forward confident, equipped, and unshaken, knowing that **"in all these things we are more than conquerors through Him who loved us" (Romans 8:37, NKJV).**

A Prayer of Dedication and Victory

Heavenly Father,

I thank You for the truth, wisdom, and revelation You have poured into my life through this journey. Thank You for opening my eyes to the reality of the spiritual battle and, more importantly, to the victory I have in Jesus Christ.

I acknowledge that apart from You I can do nothing, but in Christ I am strengthened, equipped, and secure. I choose to stand firm in the authority You have given me. I renounce fear, confusion, and defeat, and I receive clarity, peace, and bold faith.

Lord, help me to daily put on the full armor of God, to remain anchored in Your Word, and to walk in obedience and discernment. Teach me to recognize the enemy's tactics and to respond not with panic, but with prayer, worship, and truth.

Fill me afresh with Your Holy Spirit. Guard my mind, my heart, my home, and my purpose. Let my life reflect Your glory, Your love, and Your power. May I walk in freedom and help others find freedom through You.

I declare that I am more than a conqueror through Christ Jesus. I walk in victory—not by my strength, but by Your grace. In Jesus' mighty name, Amen.

Commissioning: Sent in Power and Purpose

As you close this workbook, know that you are not sent out unprepared or alone. You are commissioned as **a son or daughter of God**, clothed in His righteousness, empowered by His Spirit, and anchored in His truth.

You are sent to:

- Stand firm in faith and resist the enemy

- Walk daily in obedience, humility, and courage

- Carry God's peace into places of chaos

- Speak truth where there is deception

- Pray boldly for yourself, your family, and your community

Go forward with confidence—not striving for victory, but **living from it**. The battle belongs to the Lord, and He goes before you.

"Be strong in the Lord and in the power of His might."
— Ephesians 6:10 (NKJV)

Walk in freedom.
Stand in truth.
Advance in victory.

You are commissioned—**in Christ and for His glory.**

Bibliography

Foundational & Recommended Reading

The following resources have informed and strengthened the biblical, theological, and practical foundations of this workbook. While this book is written as a ministry and training resource rather than an academic text, these works reflect trusted Christian voices whose teachings on spiritual identity, authority, deliverance, the Holy Spirit, and the role of the Church align with the principles presented throughout this workbook. Readers who desire deeper study are encouraged to explore these resources.

Anderson, N. T. (2000). *The bondage breaker.* Harvest House Publishers.
    A foundational ministry resource on identity in Christ, freedom from spiritual strongholds, and walking in truth.

Evans, T. (2011). *Victory in spiritual warfare.* Harvest House Publishers.
    Explores spiritual warfare through a Kingdom-focused lens, emphasizing Christ's authority and the believer's role in advancing God's Kingdom.

Fee, G. D. (1994). *God's empowering presence: The Holy Spirit in the letters of Paul.* Hendrickson Publishers.
    Provides theological depth on the work and presence of the Holy Spirit in the life of the believer.

Prince, D. (1998). *Spiritual warfare.* Chosen Books.
    A classic ministry work addressing deliverance, prayer, and the authority believers have in Christ.

Wagner, C. P. (1996). *Confronting the powers: How the New Testament church experienced the power of strategic-level spiritual warfare.* Regal Books.
    Examines corporate prayer, intercession, and the role of the Church in engaging spiritual conflict.